Satan Wants To Shipwreck Your Faith

May the peace of God rest upon you and fill you with His wisdom as you read through this book. I pray that your spiritual eyes and ears be anointed to receive what the spirit of God would speak to you. I speak peace, contentment, faith, victory, health, joy and protection to you in Jesus' name.

Reverend James W. Hawkins, M. Th.

Satan Wants To Shipwreck Your Faith

 Unless otherwise indicated, all Scripture quotations are taken from the King James Version.

Library of Congress Cataloging-in-Publication Data

Hawkns, James
Satan Wants To Shipwreck Your Faith

ISBN 978-0-615-20893-0
Library of Congress Control Number: 2008930590

Produced by Richard Choy

For information contact:
Reverend James W. Hawkins M.Th.
2432-47 Berryville Pike
Winchester, Virginia 22603
540-662-8410 Fax 540-662-8410

Printed in the United States by Morris Publishing®
3212 East Highway 30
Kearney, NE 68847
1-800-650-7888

Contents

Acknowledgments

Thank you for the dedication and servant heart and Christ-like character of my sister, Joyce Mills, and for her faithfulness in taking the time to type this book.

Thank you to Grady Embrey for his review and editorial comments.

An extraordinary special thank you to the following people:

Ken Farley
Randy, Angel and Regan Gosnell
Grady Embrey Family
Matthew Knight Family
Albert Iden Elsea
Rev. Luther & Betty Foster

Dedication

To my Mother and Father:
Delsie Pearl Hawkins and Andrew Warren Hawkins

To my wonderful wife of 44 years Rev. Christine Ruth Hawkins, who has been one of the guiding forces of encouragement to press me on, to keep the faith, and always telling me you can do it and we will make it.

And our three wonderful children:

Andrew, Katherine and Susan

Foreword

I am writing to increase your confidence in God and His Word and to also encourage you and strengthen you in the faith. I use real life experiences, as encouragements to the ordinary person, the least, the lonely and the lost, to show that God is no respecter of persons. With Him, what He will do for me, He will do for you. This book is not intended to be a masterpiece, but to be one of comfort and encouragement. "And I, Brethren, when I came to you, I came not with excellency of speech or of wisdom, declaring unto you the testimony of God." (I Corinthians 2.1)

This book is not about naming it and claiming it, but is about true faith you need in order that your faith doesn't get shipwrecked. It provides important information on spiritual armor, spiritual warfare, prayer, renewing of the mind, nine Gifts of the Spirit, and Fruit of the Spirit. Faith is not a VISA or American Express card. Faith is action. Faith is trust. Faith is a walk. Faith is about believing and obeying.

In order to receive the promise, there are requirements and conditions that have to be met in order to receive the promise. Example: See Mark 11:24-25. Discipleship, prayer, dying to one's self, fasting, obedience, and to humble yourself. Holiness, repentance, spiritual armor, and renewing of the mind will help withstand the storm of life so your faith won't be shipwrecked.

1

The Storm at Sea and Your Anchors

The Storm at Sea and Your Anchors

I Timothy 1:19 Holding faith, and a good conscience; which some having put away concerning faith have made shipwreck.

I Peter 4:12 Beloved think it not strange concerning the fiery trial which is to try you, as though some strange thing happened unto you.

Luke 22: 31-32 And the Lord said "Simon, Simon, behold, Satan hath desired to have you that he may sift you as wheat, but I have prayed for thee, that thy faith fail not."

Satan wants to shipwreck your faith.

Acts 27: The storm at sea and God's anchors. (Verses: 14-44)

Faith that works no matter what kinds of problems comes our way. Your back is against the wall; anchor your faith in God!

<u>The Storm at Sea</u>

Paul got a word from God telling him "Don't Go," but the ship's captain wouldn't listen. The storm hit the boat, and it fell apart. When the storms of life hit us, it is not the time to fall apart.

Paul, this little Holy Ghost preacher (Verse 25) says "Be of good cheer." It seems like he was crazy. Be of good cheer, man it's a storm going on. This little Holy Ghost preacher said "for I believe God." Satan might shipwreck this boat, but not my faith. It shall be even as He told me. The world today is looking for men and women of God to stand and say in the midst of the storm, it's going to be all right, praise God. There is a way out of your troubles. There is a way out of your sickness. There is a way out of your financial problems. There is a way out for that flesh problem you might have, to control the door of your lips, and that is Jesus.

Verse 29: I want you to look at different anchors you cast out in the midst of the storm. Faith is an action.

(Verse 22) Be of good cheer, no loss of life.

(Verse 23) Whom I serve. (Verse 24) God has given. Base your faith in God. Keep your eyes on Him.

Psalms 121:1: I will lift up my eyes unto the hills from whence cometh my help. My help cometh from God which made heaven and earth.

God moves mountains, prayer moves God. Folks, to get the victory, right in the midst of your storm, we must affirm (confess) that God is able and God will see me through! Devil - you are a liar. What we believe in our hearts must be said. We have to let the devil know how we stand.

Verse 37: Paul was outnumbered by 276 sailors on that boat. He stood up and said I believe God. Some of you are even afraid to offer prayer over your food in a restaurant. Isn't that true? I can tell you from my own experiences that it pays to pray over your meals.

My wife and I, along with our three children, were traveling. The Holy Sprit told me to stop at a Ponderosa Steak House and eat. I prayed to God as I wanted to make sure He wanted us to stop there, knowing what little funds we had. As I pulled into the Ponderosa parking lot, my wife said "Jimmie, are you sure?" I said "Yes, get whatever you want to eat." As we were waiting in line, the kids said, "Can we get whatever we want?" I said "Sure go ahead." Oh, if you could have only seen the look on my wife's face. Perhaps a look of wonder or thinking to herself, am I going to have to wash dishes? I said "Honey, it's going to be alright." We got our food and sat down at the table to eat. We always hold hands and pray over our meals. As we started eating, I looked over at my wife and told her to enjoy her meal. The place was packed. About half way through our meal, I happened to look up and saw an old man walking on a cane coming across the room. He came to our table and said to me "I am a senior citizen. I come here often to eat and I watch and see who prays over their meal and sadly very few people do." He said, "Your family has really blessed me, so I want to pay for your family's meal." I said, "Thank you, Lord." I looked over at my wife and could see a smile of relief on her face. Again, I say it pays to pray over your meals!

Verse 35: Here Paul stands and affirms what's in his heart. It looks like there is no way out. Only a man or woman of God can do and say this. In a storm, I believe God - you don't have to have a big crowd to go along with you.

Matthew 18:19: "Again I say unto you that if two of you shall agree on earth as touching anything that they shall ask, it shall be done for them of my Father which is in heaven." Verse 20: "For where two or three are gathered together in my name there am I in the midst of them." You've got to say what you believe so that the devil will see you believe different from what he is doing! He might have you against the wall, trying to shipwreck your faith, but the fight isn't over yet.

Speak the Word of God to the devil. The answer is

on the way. Hallelujah!

I am talking about a faith that works. When you are feeling pain, you can look at the devil and say "By His stripes, I am healed." God is not going to disappoint that kind of faith. Look at Verse 29 - Four anchors they cast out to use - it is the same today - you have to have anchors to keep from drifting on life's sea or you will be tossed to and fro.

The Storm at Sea and God's Anchors

Hebrews 6:18-20: Two anchors of the soul being both sure and steadfast.

First Anchor: An anchor which is impossible - is for God to tell a lie. If He spoke it, He will bring it to pass. Numbers 23:19: "God is not a man that He would lie." II Corinthians 1:20: "For all the promises of God in Him are yea, and in Him amen, unto the glory of God by us."

I Kings 8:56: "According to all that He has promised: There hath not failed one word of all His good promises." I am trying to get your eyes on Jesus.

Verse 29: They cast out 4 anchors.

Verse 24: The fulfillment of His will in our lives. Paul said "Let the storms blow, I know which way I am going." An Angel said "I was going before Caesar," and that's the way we ought to be, and say what He says. It takes faith to say I don't care what the devil says, I am going over to the other side. Praise God. This is the fulfillment of these promises. There is a will of God in your life. Nobody can do what God wants you to do. He is depending on you to lower your anchor in Him and raise your sight on Him. I will lift up mine eyes unto the hills whence cometh my help. God is depending on you just like you are depending on Him.

Isaiah 43:1&2: "I have redeemed thee. I have called thee by thy name: thou are mine." When thou passest through the water, I will be with thee and through the rivers they shall not overflow thee. When thou walkest through the fire, thou should not be burned; neither shall the flames kindle upon thee."

Satan wants to shipwreck your faith. He hath desired to have you that he may sift you as wheat but Jesus has prayed for thee - thy faith fails not.

God said I have called you. I have found you. I have picked you up out of that mess and He said I got a job for you to do. Let's get on with it. An example of this is just like when He picked Saul of Tarsus up off of the road on his way to Damascus. In Acts 9:4: He said, "Saul, Saul why persecuted me, I got a job for you to do!"

Arise go into the city. I'll tell you what to do. Thank God for history. Thank God for His Word. It tells us what has happened and what's going to happen. Thank God for the Holy Ghost teaching and guiding us.

Acts 27:23: An Angel of God stood by me. Someone said, If only I just had an Angel to stand beside of me. Who wants an Angel, when you have Him? Him - "Greater is He that is in you than he that is in the world." (I John 4:4) We have Him and His Word for anchors. The story was told that somebody was dying. They were gathered around her and she said the Angels were coming to get her. She rose up off of the bed and said "No, no Angel is coming to carry me home. Jesus is."

The Fulfillment of His Will, It's got To Come to Pass - Nobody Can Stop It!

Second Anchor: I Kings 8:56: "Blessed be the Lord, that hath given rest to His people Israel, according to all that He promised, which He promised by the hand of Moses His servant."

The Strength of His Power

Third Anchor: Matthew 28:18: Jesus is back from that grave - He said all power is given to me in Heaven and in Earth. You and I are on the winning side and His power is available to us.

Acts 1:8: "But you shall receive power after that the Holy Ghost is come upon you."

The Availability of His Power Given to Us

He saved us so He could fill us with His power. Luke 10:19: "Behold I give unto you power to tread on serpents and scorpions and over all the power of the enemy and nothing shall by any means harm you." That anchor of power He has given us. In my name, signs and wonders will follow you. In my name, they shall cast out devils. In my name you will lay hands on the sick and they shall recover. Power that anchor of power He has given us.

Acts 28: 3-5: Miracle of the Viper Bite Paul had gathered a bundle of sticks, laid them on the fire and a viper came out of the heat fastening on his hand. He shook off the beast into the fire. Paul felt no harm. (A viper is a type of snake.) The snake bit into the power and died. The snake had to let go.

Notice he shook off the beast into the fire. Paul felt no harm. I want to tell you there are some things you have to shake off: discouragement, doubt, fear, unforgiveness, bitterness, jealousy, resentment, sadness, etc. Just like Paul, you will feel no harm, no hindrance in getting your prayers answered. By applying the applications of shaking off these different entities, and dealing with the root of the problems, a healing will take place and you will experience no harm.

You have the power. The anchor of power - put that power to work to change the situation around you.

You're going to have to speak His Word.

Anchor: The Unfailing Promises of His Word

Fourth Anchor: II Corinthians 1:20: "For all the promises of God in Him is yea, and in Him Amen, unto the glory of God by us."

"Blessed be the Lord, that hath given rest to His people Israel, according to all that He promised. There hath not failed one word of all His good promises which He promised by the hand of Moses His servant." (I Kings 8:56)

John 15:7: "If yea abide in me, and my words abide in you, ye shall ask what ye will, and it shall be done unto you."

The unfailing promises of His Word!

You can deposit it in the bank, you can stand on it. His Word is faithful!

If it's in the Book, God will fulfill it. The power of His Word is when we speak it. You don't have to shake it down. You don't have to jump it down. Oh I feel it now, goose bumps from head to toe. This Word is not based on your feelings. For we walk by faith not by feeling or by sight.

What I am trying to get you to see is, you have it, He abides in you, and He lives here in these temples.

I Corinthians 6:19: "What know ye not that your body is the temple of the Holy Ghost which is in you, which ye have of God, and are not your own."

Acts 27:29: When we are in a storm, there are anchors we need to cast out.

The Promise of His Abiding Presence

Fifth Anchor: Anchor of power that is living on the inside of you.

Matthew 28:20: "Lo I'm with you always even unto the end of the world."

Hebrews 13:5: "I will never leave thee nor forsake thee."

I said His abiding presence - He doesn't visit you like some of you visit church. Say ouch if you can't say amen!

Believe and speak His Word knowing the anchor of His abiding presence.

The Anchor of Faith

Sixth Anchor: Acts 27:32: Then the soldiers cut off the ropes of the boat and let her fall off. Faith is action, cut off other avenues. In Verse 30, they had dropped the life boat into the water. In Verse 31, Paul said, "Except these abide in the ship ye cannot be saved."

Depend on God. Paul said, "If you are going to be saved you must stay in the ship." Today if you are going to be saved, you have to abide in the Word.

If you are going to be saved, you have to abide in the church. Hebrews 10:25 "...not forsaking the assembling of ourselves together." If you are saved, you will want to do for Him.

Witnessing, laying hands on the sick and doing His will. God said stay in the ship but - the ship is going down. Hold fast.

<u>This Is the Anchor of Our Security</u>

Seventh Anchor: In Him, it took courage for Paul to say what he did. Sometimes it takes courage to stay and not move, and it takes courage to stand and not run. We are sheep. "The Lord is my shepherd. I shall not want." (Psalm 23) You see, it's the shepherd's job to take care of the sheep. He leads you in green pastures. While lurking all around you are raving wolves, with one thing on their minds - lamb chops!

That thief that comes to steal, rob, and destroy.

Isn't that right? You're trying to do what is right.

Now all that the devil can do is growl. You hear him and look to the Shepherd. He takes care of you. He is the anchor of our security. You don't have to worry, you have a shepherd that knows how to take care of his sheep and He said I will abide with you forever.

In the midst of your shipwreck, what are you to do? Look at this - Acts 27:35..."right in the middle of all this, He took bread and gave thanks to God in the presence of them all." What a message, in the middle of it all, He stopped and gave thanks.

Right in the middle of the mess, you can say Thank You, Jesus, because you know what the outcome is going to be. He has it under control. Thank you Jesus, thank you Jesus. Faith always works!

Paul had a spirit of thanksgiving. Some folks don't have that today! Some say I'll thank Him after I get it. THEN I'LL THANK HIM! We have got to learn to thank God. Paul said be thankful in all things. Now how can you be thankful in all things? Good question! By anticipating results, expect it to happen. Expect Him to bring it to pass. Psalm 30:5: "Sorrow may endure for the night but joy is coming in the morning." It may look like in your shipwreck you are trapped now but this fight isn't over.

You are the victor, not the <u>victim</u>; you are not the one that's going to be overcomed. Because of His presence, you are more than a conqueror. Greater is He that is in you then he that is in the world.

This is what He is talking about; you don't thank Him after the fact, but before! Real faith, knows how to thank Him in the midst of the crisis.

Remember God when He came to Lazarus' grave. "He prayed Father; I thank thee that thou hast heard me (expecting, confidence)." (I John 5:14)

<u>The Anchor of Security</u>

II Corinthians 1:20: "For all the promises of God, in Him are yea and in Him amen, unto the glory of God by us."

I Kings 8:56: "Blessed be God, that hath given rest to His people Israel, according to all that He promised. There hath not failed one word of all His great promises, which He promised by the hand of Moses His servant."

Acts 27:44: "And the rest, some on boards and some on broken pieces of the ship, and so it came to pass, that they escaped all safe to land."

God used the broken pieces to get them to shore. When Satan tries to shipwreck, use the anchor of security. My wife Christine and I flew to Connecticut in 1993 in the winter time. It was snowing when we went and it was snowing when we came back. On arriving back at Dulles Airport, we had to circle many times. The captain came on and announced they were experiencing difficulty with the landing gear not working. The stewardess informed us as to what position to get in. While the plane circled to burn up fuel, I took notice of everyone's actions. Some read the paper, some were fearful. I grabbed my wife's hand and said let's pray. We had prayed before we left for a safe trip. Psalms 121:8: "God shall preserve thy going out and thy coming in from this time forth and even for ever more." As I started praying, I was reminded of the promise God had given me that I would go to the nations. Just before I had started to pray, my wife looked out of the window and saw the pads and cushions on the runway, fire trucks, and ambulances beside the runway, for we were going in for a belly landing. In the middle of my prayer, I reminded God and told my wife of his promises concerning the nations. I let go of her hand and said "It will be alright." About that time we went in for a landing. The landing gear started working. Praise God, sometimes He doesn't come real early, but never, never too late!! Security of his Word ...Acts 27:44...God used broken pieces to get them to shore. There are a lot of broken pieces in people's lives in this world. God can use your broken life, your broken heart, or your broken home. God loves to pick up broken pieces and put them back together to get you to the other side. <u>The fulfillment of His will, the anchor of His power, the anchor of our security and the anchors of His abiding presence.</u> God said my body was broken for you. It was broken to set you free. The storms and the right anchors are there to use when Satan is trying to shipwreck your faith.

Is your life shipwrecked today? Broken in pieces? Are you anchored in God? Has your ship sailed the wrong sea? Have you backslidden because of having no anchors? No anchors of the fulfillment of His will in your life. No anchors of His power? No anchors of His security of Him being with you always. Some of you as you are reading this book realize that things are not right with God. You can make things right by using I John 1:9: "If you confess your sins, He is faithful and just to forgive our sins and to cleanse us from all unrighteousness." Psalm 103:12: "As far as the east is from the west so far has He removed our sins from us."

Isaiah 43:25: "I even I, am He that blotted out thy transgressions, for mine own sake and will not remember thy sins."

How to Receive Christ:

1. Admit your need - I am a sinner.
2. Be willing to turn from your sins. Repent.
3. Believe that Jesus died for your sins on the cross and rose from the grave.
4. Through prayer, invite Jesus to come in and control your life through the Holy Spirit.
5. Receive Him as your Lord and Savior.

How to Pray:

Lord Jesus, I know that I am a sinner and need your forgiveness.

I believe that you died for my sins.

I want to turn from my sins. I now invite you to come into my heart and life.

I want to trust you as Savior and follow you as Lord.

Romans 10:13: "For whosoever calls upon the name of the Lord shall be saved."

Luke 15:10: "There's joy in heaven over one sinner that repented." Praise God.

How to Receive Christ

1. Admit your need (I am a sinner).
2. Be willing to turn from your sins (Repent).
3. Believe that Jesus died for your sins on the cross and rose from the grave.
4. Through prayer, invite Jesus to come in and control your life through the Holy Spirit.
5. (Receive him as your Lord and Savior.)

How to Pray

Lord Jesus, I know that I am a sinner and need your forgiveness.

I believe that you died for my sins.

I want to turn from my sins. I now invite you to come into my heart and life.

I want to trust you as Savior and follow you [illegible].

Scripture [illegible] whosoever calls upon the name of the Lord shall be saved!

[illegible] repented [illegible].

2

Holding Faith and a Good Conscience

Holding Faith and a Good Conscience

Which some having put away concerning faith have made shipwreck.

This man Paul had faith in all things he went through. II Corinthians 1:24: "For by faith ye stand." II Corinthians 5:7: "For we walk by faith not by sight." Hebrews 11:6: "But without faith it is impossible to please Him for he that cometh to God must believe that He is, and that He is a rewarder of them that diligently seek him."

This man Paul's anchor of security - Romans 8:35-39: "Who shall separate us from the love of Christ, shall tribulation or distress or persecution, or famine or nakedness or peril, or sword."

36. "As it is written, for thy sake we are killed all the daylong; we are counted as sheep for the slaughter.

37. Nay in all things we are more than conquerors through Him that loved us.

38. I am persuaded that neither death, nor life, nor angels, nor principalities, nor powers, nor things present, nor things to come.

39. Nor height, nor depth, nor any other creature, shall be able to separate us from the love of Jesus which is in Christ Jesus our Lord."

Paul said in II Corinthians 11:24-27: He had been beaten with 39 stripes, been beaten with rods, and he was stoned 3 times. He suffered shipwreck, a night and a day; I have been in the deep. He was in perils of robbers, in perils with his country men, in perils in the wilderness, in perils in the sea, and in perils among the false brethren. He was in weariness and painfulness, in hunger and in thirst. Peter would say as, Paul, (I Peter 4:12) "Beloved, think it not strange concerning the fiery trials, which, is to try you, as though some strange thing happened unto you." Peter knew that Satan would try to shipwreck your faith. But no matter what, Paul said in Romans 8:28: "And we know that all things work together for good to them that love God, to them who are called according to His purpose." Paul says there's no way we can stop all the shipwrecks that come our way. However, you can be prepared for them in order to stand when Satan tries to shipwreck our faith. How?

The world today is looking for Christians who can stand up to every crisis. No matter what fear, trouble, or difficulty comes their way, Christians should remain calm and at rest in the midst of it all.

The world needs to see God's children trusting wholly in their God. The world must be able to point to a Christian and say, "They have something that I want. There goes one who isn't a complainer - he doesn't fret or fear or run in time of trouble."

He isn't worried about tomorrow. Whether you know it or not, you are witnessing and confessing every day to those around you, your family, your brothers and your sisters in the Lord.

They see you going through a difficult time. They watch you and they listen. Then they say to themselves, "Will they live what they preach to others when they are going through shipwreck?"

Will their Jesus let them down? What do those around you hear coming from your lips when things get tough? What do they hear and see from us? Continued sadness is a terrible confession for a believer.

Paul kept the faith no matter what came his way. When are you going to reach that place?

I Timothy 1:19: "Holding faith, and a good conscience; which some having put away concerning faith have made shipwreck." Some have given up. Some have fallen by the wayside. Some have their faith overthrown. Jesus prayed for Peter that his faith wouldn't be shipwrecked. Luke 22:31: And the Lord said, "Simon, Simon, behold, Satan hath desired to have you, that he might sift you as wheat."

32. But I have prayed for thee that thy faith fail not: and when thou art converted, strengthen thy brethren."

Peter, you and I, know it is going to take Genesis to Revelation and living all 66 books of the Bible to make it to Heaven. Satan desires you. He desires to shipwreck your faith. Jesus said, "I pray that my faith fail not." Satan is trying to sift our faith. He is trying so hard to shipwreck our faith.

I Corinthians 10:11: "Now all these things happened unto them for example and they are written for our admonition, upon whom the ends of the world are come."

Now let's look at some examples when Satan tried to shipwreck their faith. Let's see their action and what they did in the shipwreck.

Mark 4: 35-41: "And the same day, when the evening was come, he saith unto them, let us pass over unto the other side."

36. And when they had sent away the multitude, they took Him even as He was in the ship, and there were also with Him other little ships.

37. And there arose a great storm of wind, and the waves bent into the ship, so that it was not full.

38. And He was in the hind part of the ship, asleep on a pillow and they awaken him, and said unto him, Master careth not that we perish?

39. And He arose, and rebuked the wind and said unto the sea, Peace be still and the wind ceased, and there was a great calm.

40. And He said unto them, why are ye so fearful? How is that ye have no faith?

41. And they feared exceedingly and said one to another. What manner of man is this, that even the wind and the sea obey him?"

Notice Satan tried to shipwreck the <u>disciples</u> and their faith. He is trying to do the same to us today. Verse 35: <u>Should not</u> it been enough that He said let us pass over unto the other side to indicate that they would make it to the other side. Satan used a great storm of wind to beat unto the ship and fill it up with water. Notice Jesus was in the hind part of the ship sleeping away. He could sleep if he wanted to, no matter what was going on inside or outside.

My wife and I and our three children were living in Houston, Texas. A bad storm came up. The trees were close around our house. The radio had advised everyone to stay inside, tape up their windows and be prepared for damage. My wife said "Come on Jimmie and help to get prepared." I said "Honey, let's pray. God is a refuge and a fortress, and in Him, I will put my trust." When finishing our prayer, I told her I was going to lie down and go to sleep. My wife said, "What?" I said, "Everything was going to be all right."

When shipwrecks try to come, make sure that you dwell in His secret place under His shadow. Position and confession is of the utmost importance. Didn't He say no evil will befall us - that He would give his angels charge over us to keep us in all our ways? In Mark 4:37, the boat was full of water and they were looking at the circumstances instead of looking at God. It's very important where you are looking. David said in Psalm 121:1: "I will lift up mine eyes unto the hills, from whence cometh my help." Also, he said "I will direct my prayers unto thee and I will look up."

Even as some of you are reading this book, Satan is trying to shipwreck you. Don't let him! Have faith in God. Why are ye so fearful? How is it that ye have no faith? God has given us a powerful weapon to use against the enemy.

3

Our Faith

Our Faith

Hebrew 12:1: "Wherefore seeing we also are compassed about with so great a cloud of witnesses. Let us lay aside every weight, and the sin which does so easily beset us, and let us run with patience the race that is set before us.

> 2. Looking unto Jesus, the author and finisher of our faith, who for the joy that was set before Him endured the cross, despising the shame, and is set down at the right hand at the throne of God."

FAITH - GET YOUR EYES OFF THOSE FALLING AROUND YOU. SET YOUR EYES INSTEAD ON THE GREAT CLOUD OF WITNESSES WHO HAVE ALREADY MADE IT TO GLORY

1. An army of victorious brothers and sisters of all ages.

By faith, Abel, by faith, Enoch, by faith, Noah, by faith, Abraham, by faith, Jacob, by faith, Joseph, and by faith, Moses. What a great cloud of witnesses that Satan tried to shipwreck their faith but couldn't. They are in heaven cheering you and me on - those of us who are still in the race.

I can hear them off in the distance saying put away those sins. There is victory. We win. We fought even to death and didn't fall because God kept us. Hebrews 11 and 12: They are saying our faith never wavered!

Run on with patience, move forward. We are overcomers. God said, "Go on, don't quit. Your work is not in vain. I'll always go with you to strengthen and sustain." Sometimes I tell God I'm convinced I don't walk alone. But there are days when I lack courage to go on and God says don't quit. Remember I love you. Victory is just ahead and I will see you through. Winston Churchill said "Never, never, never give up."

Move Forward = Winners Never Quit

Quitters Never Win

Never waver. If you need wisdom, ask for it. James 1: 5-8: "If any of you lack wisdom, let him ask of God, that giveth to all men liberally, and upbraided not; and it shall be given him.

6. But let him ask in faith, nothing wavering, for he that wavered is like a wave of the sea driven with the wind and tossed.

7. For let not that man think that he shall receive anything of God.

8. A double minded man is unstable in all his ways." Victory amid trials and testing. Faith: The secret of answered prayer."

Don't waver; don't be moved by what's happening around you. Some might fall around you. Even a few preachers may fall - so even a few thousand preachers may fall. Those you trust may fall - that doesn't change God's Word one iota! If we don't waver, doubt and go without, believe and receive. Feed your faith, starve your doubts.

Hebrew 12:1: "Look up and see a great cloud of witnesses all decked out in white."

The devil tried to shipwreck their faith but couldn't. Ask Noah, was it worth it? All his generation fell. Only eight kept the faith, he kept the faith for 120 years in spite of all the violence, all the sin, and all of the mocking. You can overcome by the blood of the Lamb. Hold fast to your confession of the Word.

Say to that devil, you are a liar. Jesus said in John 10:10: "The thief cometh not, but for to rob, to steal, to kill and to destroy." He came to try to shipwreck your faith, don't let him!

Hebrew 11:22: The devil tried to shipwreck Joseph's faith through temptations, but his faith carried him through! God's Word says in I Corinthians 10:13: "That no temptation has taken you but such as is common to man. God is faithful. He will not suffer you to be tempted above that ye are able; but will with temptation also make a way to escape, that ye may be able to bear it." Joseph's faith carried him through.

Some of you reading this book right now have yielded to temptation. Stop right now and pray and ask Jesus to forgive you and cleanse your sins. Tell Him you are sorry for yielding to temptations, to please forgive you, that you repent of your sins, to wash you, and to clean you with the blood of Jesus. Ask for help so you will never do this again. Thank Him for the victory over temptation. I John 1:9: "If we confess our sins, He is faithful and just to forgive us our sins, and to cleanse us from all unrighteousness."

Verse 24-26 Moses: He chose to be with God's people then in Pharaoh's court. The pleasure of sin is and will be but for a short time. They must end, either in speedy repentance or in speedy ruin. <u>By faith</u> Moses, as their leader, led the Israelites as they pressed through the Red Sea on dry land. Oh the grace of faith will help us through all dangers on our way to Heaven. By faith, the servant of God shall overcome even the roaring lion that goes about seeking whom he may devour.

True Faith - example - The UPS man comes to your door. You have to open the door to receive. If you don't open the door, you do not receive.

True Faith, Trusting, Believing:

True faith is acknowledged and is accepted, even when mingled with many failures. The believer's faith endures to the end.

Even in dying, gives him victory over death and all his deadly enemies.

Don't let the devil shipwreck your faith. That's why some folks are not in church today.

What you are going through as a Child of God is no accident. Every test, every fiery trial is under His careful, watchful eyes and there is purpose to it all. Brothers and Sisters don't faint. Don't cast away your faith (confidence). Satan is a liar.

Hebrews 12:1 "The cloud of witnesses cries out to get back into the battle and fight with faith. Lift up the hands that hung down and strengthen the feeble knees. Don't turn aside, stay in the race and don't give up." Hold to your confidence in the Word. Satan tried to shipwreck Paul's faith many, many times.

In II Timothy 4:7: He said, "I have fought a good fight, I have finished my course. I have kept the faith!" He kept the faith in the good times and in the bad times. Acts 20:24: "But none of these things move me." That's why he could boast. I have fought a good fight. I have finished my course. I have kept the faith. How about you, can you say the same as Paul? Paul received 39 stripes five times. He said "Hey I have been in prison so many times, beaten with rods 3 times, man I have been stoned. I have been robbed, even by my own brothers. Oh, but I kept the faith. Satan didn't shipwreck my faith." Paul said "I have been so weary at times, full of pain, sleepless nights, hungry, thirsty, cold, loaded down with cares of all kinds, yet I kept the faith." He said "I have been troubled, distressed, persecuted but never cast down, never destroyed, never shaken in my faith!" Satan tried to shipwreck my faith. He tried to shipwreck those brothers and sisters in Hebrews 11, but couldn't. He is defeated for he is a liar - the father of lies; he can't shipwreck your faith today if you don't let him. Oh he might try with discouragement, sickness, or problems, but he is a defeated fool because greater is He that is in you then he that is in the world.

God, I pray for the one who is reading this book. All the trials and tests they are going through that they can see the different ones in this book as to what they went through, who kept the faith and didn't allow Satan to shipwreck their faith.

4

The Anchor of Our Faith

The Anchor of Our Faith

"But without faith, it is impossible to please Him; for he that cometh to God must believe that He is and that He is a rewarder of them that diligently seek Him." (Hebrews 11:6) "So then faith cometh by hearing and hearing comes by the Word of God." (Romans 10:17) "Watch ye, stand fast in the faith, quit you like men, and be strong." (I Corinthians 16:13) In other words, be men of courage. "Now faith is the substance of things hoped for, the evidence of things not seen." (Hebrews 11:1) "For by faith ye stand." (II Corinthians 1:24) " For we walk by faith, not by sight." (II Corinthians 5:7)

Faith will make the difference of how you approach daily circumstances and crises in your life, and the outcome of these trials and tests you face. Faith only grows when you use it. Life can be a stepping stone or a stumbling block. It's your choice to react or respond. I am going to respond with the Word. I have been knocked down many times. "Many are the afflictions of the righteous but the Lord delivers him out of them all." (Psalms 34:19) You see we know that the tests sometimes will knock us down, but we don't have to stay down!!

We are in warfare with the Prince of the Air. To keep from staying down, we have to apply our faith, be persistent, discipline, have determination, endurance, and durability and hold fast and stand and fight God's fight of faith. Trusting, being obedient, and keeping our eyes on Jesus, the author and finisher of our faith. (Hebrews 12:2)

Faith's experiences in my life in which Satan tried and tested me to shipwreck my faith and thoughts that Satan tries to inject in our minds include:

- Thoughts of despair
- Thoughts of discouragement
- Thoughts of you can't do it
- Thoughts of you won't make it
- Thoughts of you are a failure and
- Thoughts of all kinds of things to shipwreck your faith.

Faith's Experience in My Life

Please bear in mind these examples are not meant for any self exaltation but to encourage you to have faith and stand on The Word of Faith!

In the summer of 2005, I was using a riding mower cutting grass. After about four hours of cutting grass, I was on a steep hill next to a creek. I started cutting at this one place backing up to the creek. As I got right to the edge and applied the brakes, it would not work. I went backwards on the lawnmower and down a seven foot embankment. It threw me and the lawnmower across to the other side, with the mower landing on me. I don't know to this day how that lawnmower cut off, but it stopped running just before it landed on my leg. An angel had to have cut it off. Satan tried to shipwreck my faith and my physical body. I had 4 broken ribs on one side and six fractured ribs on the other side, plus a big black bruise on my side and on my back. I laid there with the lawnmower on my leg submerged in the edge of the creek with smoke coming from the mower, along with gas running down the side of it.

I was down in a hole where no one could see me. I prayed and I quoted "Call upon me in the day of trouble." (Psalm 50:15) Then I began to shout real loud and after a while, a man heard me. He came and looked at me and I told him to go next door and get help. It took three men to lift the mower off of me. While I was lying there, the devil said, "I am going to kill you." I said, "I rebuke and resist you in the name of Jesus." You see he tried to shipwreck my faith by telling me no one would see or find me, and that it was over. My wife took me to the hospital where we found out my condition. She then took me home to recuperate from the accident. As I lay in bed, I quoted: "For I will restore health unto thee and I will heal thee of thy wounds," saith the Lord. (Jeremiah 30:17) "Many are the afflictions of the righteous but the Lord delivered him out of them all." (Psalms 34:19) I said Master you said "If thou can'st believe all things are possible to Him that believeth." (Mark 9:23) I said "Master, it's by your stripes I am healed." I could hardly move or walk but I responded with the Word, and by praising Him and thanking Him for healing me. "For we walk by faith, not by sight." (II Corinthians 5:7) Praise His Holy Name. Fight the good fight of faith so that Satan won't shipwreck your faith.

Faith Experience in My Life

The experience of falling off a double wide modular home in the winter of 2004 - It had been raining, snowing and sleeting for days. All of a sudden, over one window, water was leaking in real bad. I couldn't get anyone to repair it, so I got the material to fix it myself. I climbed up the ladder to get on top of the roof. I stepped one foot onto the ladder, and walked across the roof to the window which was leaking water into the inside. I broke the ice, cleaned over top of the window and applied the material. I walked back to the ladder to get off of the double wide. As I stepped one foot on to the ladder, it was like a whirl wind had turned the ladder around, throwing me backwards for over five feet. I landed on the top of the handrail, sliding down the hand rail with my head first, on to my back. I went fifteen feet, fell off, and was knocked unconscious for a while. When I came to, I couldn't walk, so I crawled back to our

home to lay on the bed until my wife came home.
She took me to the hospital and thought I was going to die on the way. At the hospital, they put me in the trauma room, ran all kinds of tests and found out that I had broken ribs and bad bruises all over my body. The doctors said somebody must have been watching over me to come out of this fall as well as I did. Satan tried to shipwreck my faith, but he couldn't do so, as the Lord kept me through it all.

Faith Experience in My Life

In the month of December after Christmas, my wife and I went to visit our daughter Kathy and her family in Maryland. My wife and I were unloading the car, and carrying in our belongings as we were going to spend the night. At their front door was a small porch, with three steps. I carried some things in the house but I had to go back outside. As I opened the door, I stepped down on the small porch, losing my footing. I fell head first down the steps, across the sidewalk, landing on the sidewalk, and rolled over onto the grass. I thought I was going to pass out. I laid there for a while, and then got up just as my wife was coming out the door. She saw me getting up and asked me what happened. I told her as I went into the house to lie on the bed. She said, "Let's go to the emergency room.' I said, "No this time, they can't really do anything for me." I felt like I had broken several ribs. I was in a lot of pain with big bruises on my side. I said, "Let's just trust the Lord for the healing," as my wife and family had done so many times before. Again the enemy tried to shipwreck my faith.

Faith Experience in My Life

In 2004, I was having severe pain in my right side as we were getting ready to go to India. I went to see Dr.Ulich, and after examining me, he told me my gallbladder had to come out. He said it would be a simple surgery; but, it didn't go that way. The plan was to make a small incision and as he did, I began to bleed extensively. At that point, it became a major operation in which they had to prop up my liver. At that point, he wasn't sure he could bring me through the operation. I praise God for a good Christian doctor and for the many saints praying for me. At the time of my operation, our friend, Mary Bauer in North Carolina, was praying for me and she saw a vision of angels in an operating room bringing peace to a chaotic scene. She then knew it was me being operated on and prayed more fervently for both me and the doctor. "With God nothing is impossible" (Luke 1:37) so again, Satan tried to shipwreck my faith, and even tried to kill me through the operation.

Faith Experience in My Life

We had fasted and prayed for our trip to India, the money had come in, the meetings were lined up and everything was set to go. All of a sudden, I began to run a high fever. I said, "By faith, we are going." We went to the airport as I knew we were supposed to go even though the enemy didn't want us to go. I got on the plane and got real sick with a high fever again. We prayed and said we are still going. We were praying, and I started to feel better. We had fourteen hours in flight to Germany, and then had a three hour layover before continuing for another fourteen hour flight to India. We stayed fourteen days and we had a wonderful time as Pastor Paul Masilaman is a special man of God. We had meetings at his church and at several other churches in which we saw several outstanding miracles take place. One miracle in particular, the Lord healed a woman who had a bad back problem for over a year. Praise His Name! I was in the best of health the whole time I was there. We went back to India for a meeting the following year also. "My Lord healeth me of all my disease." (Psalm 103.3)

Faith Experience in Our Lives

Our son, Andy, was about seven years old and was having trouble seeing. We took him to an eye doctor. After he examined him, the doctor said he was eighty percent blind in one eye and was going blind in the other one. We began to pray and intercede for our son's eyes. Several months went by with no improvement. We were standing on the Word by faith. A friend told us about a Pentecostal church in Manassas, Virginia, where they laid hands on the sick and prayed for people. We went to the church but they didn't pray for the sick at that service. After the service was over, the preacher's wife noticed our son was wearing glasses. She laid hands on him and he almost fell backwards when the power of God hit him. She said "Son, you are too young to be wearing glasses - be healed in the name of Jesus." Andy said, "I felt the Lord heal me."

We praised the Lord. Now you can be sure the devil said real low - he's not healed. We said Devil you are a liar - he is healed. The next week we went to Kings Dominion.

We were walking around and went into this one shop. A woman was crawling around on the floor saying don't come over here because I dropped my contact lenses on the floor. We stood there for a minute and Andy asked me what she was looking for. I said small contact lenses you wear like glasses - it is a real small plastic-like piece. We were standing there for a minute or so and Andy walked over about three or four feet, bent down, picked up the contact lenses and said Daddy is this she is looking for? I said yes son, give it to that woman. Not only did the Lord heal, but he increased his sight. Years later Andy went into the Air Force and was stationed at McGuire Air Force Base in New Jersey. Andy got orders to go to the horn of Africa. He called me and told me this. I said son I don't get a good witness to that, you are not supposed to go. Andy said Dad you don't understand I have orders - I am on twenty four hour stand-by to leave. My wife and I went immediately in prayer and fasting. The next day Andy called us and said, Mom, Dad, my orders have been cancelled. "For I am the Lord - I changed not." (Malachi 3:6) I want to tell you as you read this book, God moves mountains. Prayer moves God, faith pleases God. For what He has done for me, He will do for you. "For there is no respecter of persons with God." (Romans 2:11) I pray as you read these faith experiences in my life; you will be encouraged, and strengthened in the Lord no matter what you are going though. Read what he has done for my wife and children and me. Later on, we carried Andy to another doctor to examine him and he said his eyes were excellent - with perfect vision! Praise the Lord!

Faith Experience in Our Lives

We were living in Bealeton, Virginia with our children, and they were going to a Christian school close by. One day one of the children was at our house playing with our youngest daughter Susan (Susie) while I was gone. Susie was playing in the yard bouncing on a pogo stick, jumping up and down. Some way or the other it came up and hit her in the eye. She came into the house, and when my wife saw her eye, she immediately prayed for her. Susie was screaming uncontrollably, so my wife asked all the children who were there to lay hands on her and pray for her. Then the peace of God came upon her. The next day Susie had to go to school, so she asked us if she could wear a covering over her eye. We said yes. In about a week her eye was completely healed. Everyone was amazed about her miracle. Satan tried to cripple Susie and shipwreck her faith and ours. "If thou canst believe, all things are possible to him that believeth." (Mark 9:23)

Faith Experience in Our Lives

The experience of our daughter Katherine (Kathy)'s heart murmur. The doctors were going to operate and replace a valve in her heart. They told Kathy what had to be done. She said okay as she didn't realize the extent or seriousness of what they had to do until they told her they would have to break her ribcage, and cut her from her shoulder to her waist. Then she said I want to pray about this. After we had all prayed, she went back for the pre-op preparation in which another x-ray was taken. The original heart problem could not be found. The doctors checked and checked and thought perhaps a mistake had been made, and then they said they could not find a heart murmur. Praise the Lord! Satan tried to kill her and destroy her and our faith. "He healeth the broken in heart, and bindeth up their wounds." (Psalms 147:3)

Faith Experience in Our Lives

The Experience of Going to Texas - The Holy Spirit spoke to me about going to Texas. When I told my wife, she said, "Jimmie, you are crazy." I told her the Lord had confirmed it to me several times for us to go. I said, "You had better pray about it," and she did. After a while, the Lord confirmed it to her as well. We packed up some of our things and left for Texas. We had enough money for gas and food and some for a month's rent, or so we thought. We went by faith to Texas. I said, "Where Lord? Texas is mighty big." Go to Houston, the Holy Spirit confirmed. Just as we got into Texas, a town called Orange, Texas, I saw a sign advertising a Women's Aglow Meeting. The Holy Spirit told us to go to that meeting. They had dinner before the meeting began. I said we are just going to the meeting. A man and woman was sitting over to the side of the room, they jumped up and said that the Lord told them to pay for our dinners. We ate and then waited for the meeting to start. The speaker was a woman prophetess. During the meeting, she called me out and asked me to stand up. She then prophesied things over me that only God knew about. After the meeting, she came up to us and said to me, "When I first saw you, I started to say something exactly the opposite of what I prophesied. At first I was in the flesh." Just as were about to leave, a man and a woman came up and said, "We have never done this before. The Holy Spirit said to give them a check." So she said, "Here is a check for ten dollars from my husband and me." We went from there to Houston. We arrived to find out there were four lanes of traffic going each way. With a feeder road, you had to turn off to get to side roads or streets. I told my wife "Let's get out of here." We went back to Louisiana and spent the day. The next night praying, I couldn't sleep because I was out of the will of God. The Holy Spirit said get back to Houston, so we left early the next morning for Houston. As we arrived there, I was driving around looking for a place to rent. We prayed and we drove around for awhile. I stopped and pulled over and prayed, "Lord where is our place at?" As we were praying, the Holy Spirit said turn at the next road to the right and go down that road. We drove just a little way, and then there was a street going to the left. Just as we were going by it, there was a trailer on the left. The owner was in the front yard with a hammer and a sign, indicating it was for rent. We stopped and I talked to the owner. He showed us the trailer that had no furniture. He said, "I like you and your family so I will rent it to you. You can pay me the first month's rent and spread the deposit over the next three months." We said, "Praise the Lord as all we have is the first month's rent." The water and electric was on and he said we could change that later. The next day, we went to see how much it would cost to enroll our children in a Christian school. The school was starting very shortly. When my wife was talking to the principal, he offered her a job that would pay for the kid's tuition plus give her about seventy-five dollars for her. Philippians 4:19: "But my God shall supply all your needs according to his riches in glory by Christ Jesus."

Time after time, He did as He supplied our every need. God opened doors for me to preach as I was an ordained minister with the Assembly of God.

During the time we were in Houston, many trials and tests came our way with our living by faith. While we were in Houston, one day my wife and children had gone to school. I was cooking something on the stove. All of a sudden, I fell to the floor in front of the stove, my right leg had locked up and I was paralyzed. I slid on the floor and called my neighbor, and asked him to come over and cut the stove off. He cut off the stove but didn't want to leave me lying on the floor. I told him that I would be alright. I laid there for hours just praying until my wife got home. I told her what happened and I assured her I would be okay. I slid on the floor into the bedroom as I couldn't get up to walk. I was in a lot of pain. I said, "I will just sleep on the floor tonight. Tomorrow, I will be alright."

The next morning, I sent my wife and kids off to school. My wife didn't want to go. I assured her I would be okay. Well I prayed all day and quoted verses. I said I will call John Osteen and get him to come and pray for me, and the Lord will heal me. The Holy Spirit said no, I will get the glory.

My wife arrived home. She said, "Jimmie, you are still lying there. I am going to call an ambulance." Just a little while later, they arrived and took me to Ben Taub Hospital in Houston. They kept me for about a week before the MRI equipment could be fixed. Then I had the MRI which showed two ruptured disks. The doctors said all the nerves had been wrapped around my spine and had caused a pinched nerve.

They told my wife and me that I would never walk again. We prayed and asked for the Lord's will to be accomplished. I prayed, Lord you said: "Beloved, I wish above all things that thou mayest prosper and be in health, even as thy soul prospered." (II John 2) I said Lord you also said, "For I will restore health unto thee; and I will heal thee of thy wounds." (Jeremiah 30:17) I said these doctors are very knowledgeable and I praise God for them and their report. I quoted, "Who hath believed our report and to whom is the arm of the Lord revealed." (Isaiah 53:1) I said," Lord I choose to believe your report, your Word - I stand on that." I told the doctors to go ahead with the operation as everything would be alright. The operation consisted of me being cut open for seven hours and seven minutes on the operating table. After the operation, they took me to a recovery room, and then to my room, the next day. I woke up around 10:00 am. I told the nurse to call my doctor, for I wanted to go for a walk. She said, "Okay, you just lie still - don't move. I will call him." She must have thought I was flipping out or something. About an hour later, the doctor had not showed up. I asked the nurse where he was. I said, "I am going for a walk." She said, "Now just calm down, he will be here in a few minutes." I said, "Okay, I will wait a little while longer but then I will drag the IV pole with me and unplug all these wires on me." Well in a little while, the doctors came in - five of them. They said, "Mr. Hawkins you want to do what?" I told them and they said you know what we tried to tell you that you wouldn't be able to walk. I said, "Just unhook the wires and the IV pole." They just looked at me and then unhooked everything. I sat up on the bed. The bed and the room seemed to be going around and around. So I sat there for a few minutes, then got up, and walked for about seven or eight feet and looked back at the doctors. They were all standing and looking at me with their mouths wide open - as if they were in shock. I walked for about six or seven more feet and turned around and headed for the bed. The doctors said this is a miracle as there is no way that he should be walking. I laid down on the bed praising God and thanking Him, giving Him all the praise and glory. Then I said "Don't anyone touch me as I just want to rest for the next couple of days." Later on I got back up and was walking again. Just a little bit later, my wife came in the room. She said she was so blessed and surprised to see me walking after what the doctors had said. I rested and prayed and waited for my total healing from my back operation. "Said I not unto thee, if thou wouldst believe, thou shouldst see the glory of God." (John 11:40) What He has done for me, He shall do for you. Have faith. Satan did not shipwreck our faith even though it seemed like a big shipwreck in our lives.

5

The Anchor of our Faith Faith Trip Adventures in Our Lives

Again please bear in mind, these examples are not meant for any self exaltation but, to encourage you to have faith and stand on the Word by faith. "If ye abide in me, and my words abide in you, ye shall ask what ye will and it shall be done unto you." (John 15:7) Now, before we start these faith adventures, I want you to see and understand God's promises.

Someone once said the Bible has 33,300 promises. Now, I don't know that for a fact, so you read and count all the promises and see if the figure is correct and let me know. As we look at that promise in Mark 11:24, let's look at the example it shows. "Therefore I say unto you, what things so ever ye desire, when ye pray, believe that ye receive them and ye shall have them." Verse 25: "And when ye stand praying forgive, if ye ought against any: that your Father also which is in heaven may forgive you your trespasses."

I believe for every promise, there are many requirements and conditions that have to be met in order to receive the promises or answered prayers. Another example, let's look at Psalms 66:18: "If I regard iniquity in my heart, the Lord will not hear me."

Psalms 66:19: "But verily God hath heard me, He hath attended to the voice of my prayer." In writing this book about life experiences and faith adventures, is not to say just go ahead by faith, only go and do as He directs. "...and thine ears shall hear a word behind thee, saying this is the way, walk ye in it when ye turn to the right hand and when ye turn to the left." (Isaiah 30:21) "I will instruct thee and teach thee in the way which thou shalt go. I will guide thee with mine eye."(Psalm 32.8) "That the Lord thy God may show as the way wherein we may walk, and the things that we may do." (Jeremiah 42:3) "How be it this kind goeth not out but by prayer and fasting?" (Matthew 17:21) "Humble yourselves in the sight of the Lord and He shall lift you up." (James 4:10)

Notice you don't just go! In these verses are promises and examples to follow, notice first of all:

- Don't regard iniquity Psalms 66:18
- Humble yourself James 4:10
- Die to yourself Matthew 16:24
- Prayer Colossians 4:2
- Fasting Isaiah 58 and Matthew 17:21
- Holiness Hebrews 12:14 and I Peter 1:15-16
- Repentance I John 1:9
- Obedience Deuteronomy 28: The blessing of obedience.

Die to yourself, "He must increase, but I must decrease." (John 3:30) "...and He said to them all, if any man will come after me, let him deny himself, and take up his cross daily and follow me." (Luke 9:23-27) In these verses are the terms of discipleship and the cost of discipleship. We daily have to count the cost of discipleship. 1st - A choice of loyalty must be made. 2nd - A cross must be borne. 3rd - A price must be paid. In which it might be the giving up of material possessions. 4th - Jesus pointed out that a spirit of sacrifice. 5th - Giving is involved in discipleship.

Jesus said we are to take up our crosses and follow Him. His example was to live the cross life. He came to do the will of the Father. Now we don't really bear a cross literally. He gives us purpose and goals for our lives, in which we are to follow. It speaks death to self. The experience of real life is in Him. Always be ready to serve Him and live for Him. "I beseech you therefore brethren, by the mercies of God, that ye present your bodies a living sacrifice holy, acceptable unto God, which is your reasonable service." (Romans 12:1) Discipleship, prayer, die to self, fasting, obedience, humble yourselves, holiness, repentance, spiritual armor and renewing of the mind. We will deal with this in a later chapter. You have to deal with these different areas in your life. You walk in order to hear His voice giving you directions and orders so that Satan doesn't shipwreck your faith.

The Anchor of Our Faith - Faith Trip Adventures.

Please bear in mind these examples are not meant for any self exaltation, but to encourage you to have faith and stand on the Word by faith and by no means tell you to do the same thing. You only do what the Lord tells you to do - not something someone else has done. Remember faith is not a VISA or American Express card. Faith is trust, faith is an action and faith is a walk.

Faith Trip Adventure

Summer was just about over; we had done a lot of traveling and preaching in different states. School was getting ready to start. We had looked at different curriculums for home schooling. After prayer, we had narrowed it down to Calvert of Baltimore, which was geared to work with preachers, missionaries and evangelists, as we were traveling in our thirty foot motor home. One day we were all loaded in our motor home heading to Baltimore, Maryland. We were going around the beltway near Tyson's Corner, Virginia, just past where we were going north on the beltway, and cars on the other side were going south. We just happened to look over to that side when all of a sudden we saw a dump truck. The back dropped down to the road, two truck wheels came off and were headed straight toward us. It happened so fast we didn't even have time to pray. We just said, in the name of Jesus, Jesus. "Call upon me in the day of trouble, I will deliver thee, and thou shall glorify me." (Psalms 50:15) We saw those two wheels coming across the road headed right for us, hit the four to five foot divider separating the lanes, fly up into the air doing a backwards flip all the way over three lanes of the traffic and land in a field, hurting no one. Praise the Lord. Satan tried to kill us but he couldn't. He didn't shipwreck our faith but increased our faith in the Lord and His Word.

It just so happened that the next day we had to go back the same way to Maryland. This time I had a friend with us. We had told him what had happened about the dump truck wheels. Lo and behold as we got to that same place a small crane was behind the truck picking it up and the men were working on it to replace the wheels. Praise the Lord for His watchful protection. Satan tried to shipwreck our faith but the Lord wouldn't let him.

Faith Trip Adventure

We were going down Route 11 in Fredericksburg, Virginia when all of a sudden the car made a big noise. I don't remember what had happened. As we drove a little bit further, we stopped and prayed and then drove on. We saw a garage. I had enough gas to get us to where we were going. It was just my wife and I. The Holy Spirit told me to pull into that garage. I said, "Lord you know I don't have any money." This was my first experience in going to a garage with no money. The owner looked at our car and told me it had to be fixed. He said it would cost a certain amount, which I didn't have. The Holy Spirit prompted me to say go ahead and fix it. He told his mechanic what to do and my wife and I went on into the office. The owner came in and we started talking to him about the Lord and how we had been traveling for Him. He said, "Let's go into the other room" where his wife was working. He introduced us to her and as we talked for a few minutes, he said she had cancer. We told her, "My Jesus who forgiveth all thine iniquities and healeth all thy diseases can heal you." (Psalms 103:3) I asked her if we could pray for her for a healing miracle. We prayed, and she said she felt the power of God heal her. He said he also felt the presence of the Lord. We talked to her a little longer, and gave her some verses to read. We had been in there for a while. The owner had walked out to make sure our car was fixed. He came back in and said your car is fixed - there's no charge. "For my thoughts are not your thoughts, neither are your ways my ways, saith the Lord." (Isaiah 55:8) Satan tried to discourage us and shipwreck our faith by asking us what are you going to do now. We will trust God by faith.

<u>Faith Trip Adventure</u>

I cannot begin to say over the years how many times we have run out of gas and how many times we have driven while it was empty on the gas gauge. There were lots of times when we didn't have money. There were times when it was late and no gas stations were open where we were at. We should not go out in a blizzard; God has given us wisdom to know better. Now if we go out in a blizzard for some stupid reason, and perhaps it really could have waited until another day, we go against His will. He is not obligated to protect us. Now if He sends us or we are caught out in it, then that is a different story altogether. He will protect and deliver us. We were in Houston, Texas, and I had just preached a revival, some friends of ours went too. They had heard me mention about our "out of gas adventures". He asked us to go with them and for us to go in his car. We said okay and we went for a ride and we went to several places. Then he asked me to drive and I wondered why. I was driving for a while when I noticed the gas gauge was on empty. I said, "Brother we need to get some gas." He didn't say anything at first. Then he responded to me with saying, "Jimmie, this car runs out of gas when it shows the hand on empty. He said I have a lock cap on my gas tank. He said Jimmie you had better pray that we make it back to our house because I didn't bring the key." I said, "You have got to be kidding?" He said, "Hey, you said you have run out of gas and the Lord multiplied the gas before and He will do it this time." I said, "Brother this is a different situation. You told me you left the key at home on purpose. You talk about tempting the Lord." I pulled over and asked the Lord for mercy. I asked him to show this brother His power and His might just like when you fed the multitudes with a few fish and few loaves of bread. In the name of Jesus, do the same for the gas in this gas tank and He did. Praise the Lord!

I was in Culpeper, Virginia, preaching and sharing some of these experiences one night before the services and a woman came up to me and she looked very upset. She was. She said to me, "I am mad at you." I thought to myself what did I do, what did I say? She proceeded to say, "I ran out of gas today. I prayed for the Lord to multiply the gas just like you did for Jimmie Hawkins and He didn't." I said, "This was a different situation. First of all, you don't do something just because somebody else did it. You only do what the Lord tells you to do." Now we know Romans 2:11 tells us, there is no respecter of persons with God. I said, "Ma'am, let me ask you something if you don't mind." She said, "Yes." Then I said, "You could have gotten gas, couldn't you?" She bowed her head and said, "You are right. I went to a lot of places, passed a lot of gas stations. I was so busy; I said I will get gas tomorrow. I am sorry it wasn't your fault or God's fault, it was mine. Please forgive me." I said, "Let me pray for you." Saints, so many times God gets the blame for things He doesn't do. Praise God, He forgives and forgets our faults and failures. Praise God, behold I do a new thing, now it shall spring forth, shall ye not know it? I will even make a way in the wilderness and rivers in the desert. Many times in my life and yours, He has worked the impossible for me and you that are reading this book. Right now, Holy Spirit, let the readers see you are bigger than fear, any question they have, any mountain they face, any roaring sea, any need they have - you are bigger than any worries, any doubts, bigger than any need they are facing right now, bigger than any report you just received. Stop reading this book at this point, lay it down and praise Him for that. The bigness of our God, praise Him and thank Him. In Jesus name, my God is bigger than any problem. My faith will not be shipwrecked. Say what you believe, believe His Word.

The Anchor of Our Faith Experience - Faith Trip Adventures

"Neighbor, I know both how to be abased, and I know how to abound. Everywhere now in all things, I am instructed both to be full and to be hungry, both to abound and to suffer need. Not that, I speak in respect and of want: for I have learned, in whatsoever state I am, therewith to be content." (Philippians 4:11-12) Oh neighbor, if we could just learn to be content knowing "and we know that all things work together for good to them that love God, to them who are the called according to his purpose." (Romans 8:28) He allows certain things to happen to us to strengthen our faith. He tries to get us to focus on Him, to look to Him, to trust Him, and to have a dependency in Him and a relationship with Him. He wants us to see His power, His holiness, His love, His mercy, His justice, and His faithfulness.

When we lived in Virginia, one day things were very, very tight and our funds were very low. My wife and our children were sitting at the table getting ready to eat. We had a big table that could seat up to twelve people. My wife had fixed dinner for all of us; it was one big bowl of black-eyed peas. We gathered around the table to eat. I started praying, thanking the Lord for the feast that was set before us. I said, "Lord there are a lot of people today that don't have anything. We thank you for what you have given us. I thank you." " My God shall supply all our needs according to his riches in glory by Christ Jesus." (Philippians 4:19) I stopped in the middle of my prayer, and said the Holy Spirit said we were going to receive a big blessing. No sooner had I said that, than a car turned into our driveway. As we were sitting at the table eating, two women came to the door. We answered the door and said "Can I help you?" for we had never seen them before. The one woman said "The Lord said take these bags of groceries over two counties. I will tell you where you should go and the Lord said for us to come here." We told them how they were led of the Spirit to come to the right place for we were eating our last bowl of black-eyed peas. They were so happy that they listened to the Lord and then the ladies left. Satan again said see the Lord doesn't love and meet your needs. I told him, he was a liar. God does meet our needs. You see these groceries - devil? He didn't shipwreck our faith, praise God.

One day we were traveling through Elkton, Virginia. We were getting hungry so we stopped at a Pizza Hut there in Elkton. I went in and ordered a big pizza for all five of us. After a while, the pizza and drinks were ready. I had taken the children in with me to carry the drinks and pizza out to the car. When we got to the car, I set the pizza on the hood of the car. We set the drinks down. We always hold hands and pray over our food and for each other. As we were standing in front of our car praying over our food, in the middle of the prayer, our daughter Kathy said, "Dad, Dad, look!" As I turned to look, a dog jumped up and grabbed our pizza and took off running down through the woods. It must have had a lot of practice doing this.

So our daughter, Kathy was mad about this so she said "Come on Andy, Dad, we are going to tell the manager what that dog did to our pizza." I didn't say anything. I was praying and thinking, Lord what should I do now? I told Kathy and Andy to go ahead. In a few minutes, the manager came out of the door, with a gun strapped on his side. He said, "Where is that dog that took this pretty little girl's pizza?" I said that's alright as I didn't want him to shoot the dog. He turned and said, "Come with me young lady. I am going to fix you the biggest and best pizza you have ever had." The Lord never ceases to amaze us. Thank you and I praise you Lord. Your ways are higher and better than ours. (Isaiah 55:9)

The experience of praying in the money as we live by faith to make twelve trips overseas and many other trips in the states.

I could write a whole book on these trips overseas. Perhaps at a later date, I will write a book on our overseas miracles that God did. You see as we prayed, the Lord laid it on our hearts to go to these countries. We don't do like some other preachers and evangelists do and send big long mailing lists out asking for money. We pray and believe for the money, not only to go, but to be a blessing to those preachers overseas. Most of them have hardly any money or have a very small income. I want to mention just some of the highlights of a few of the trips.

We were in Germany (Ramstein at Rev. Washington's church) and the Holy Spirit moved in a special way. I had never seen this before when I gave an altar call. A bunch of men came forth running to be saved and healed. Most of the time, it is usually men and women. We had a wonderful service. Other trips included France, Haiti, Puerto Rico,

Venezuela, South America, Quito, Ecuador, Holland, Israel, England, India (twice), and Alaska. In all these trips, my point is for you to see all the places the Lord has sent my wife and me, and that He can do the same for you, if He tells you to go, He will provide. "But my God shall supply all your needs according to His riches in glory by Christ Jesus." (Philippians 4:19)

In everything you say and do, "I will lift up mine eyes unto the hills, from whence cometh my help. My help cometh from the Lord, which made heaven and earth." (Psalm 121:1-2) In all of your travels, pray this verse also. "The Lord shall preserve thy going out and thy coming in from this time forth, and even forevermore." (Psalm 121:8) So neighbor, when satan tries to shipwreck your faith, you tell him he is a liar, the Father of Lies. My God is able - just like he did for Moses, Joshua and Daniel. I don't know how, or when for you, but <u>He will do it again</u>!!

One of the great experiences of preaching was at Rev. Johnny and Betty Hensley's Upper Room Church in Elkton, Virginia. Brother Johnny (deceased) was a wonderful man of God. Johnny and Betty were two very special people, mightily used of God. Their church has a wonderful congregation who has been taught the Word of God and they love the Lord very much.

One service in particular at this church, I had preached and gave an altar call in which a lot of people came forth for prayer for different reasons. I was laying hands on people and praying for them. I came to this one man, skipped over him, and then came back to him. As I went to pray for him, the Holy Spirit said to tell him that he had a lot of money owed to him and that he would be getting it in a few days. I told him this in his ear. I didn't want to embarrass him, and I also thought it wasn't anyone else's business. After I prayed for him, he really didn't respond any differently than before I had prayed for him. I preached that night. He came up for prayer again. He didn't say anything about the prayer I had prayed for him in the previous service. Well two weeks later Brother Johnny had to be away from the church, and he asked me to preach for him. I said okay. So I went back again and preached that morning. That same man came up for prayer.

Well, just as I was ready to leave, the man was sitting down, so I walked over to tell him goodbye. He said, "Brother Jim, sit down. I want to talk to you." Remember this is the same man the Holy Spirit had said was going to get his money. Had he got it back or not? My mind flashed back to remember when I was in North Carolina preaching. Church had started and it was time for me to start preaching. The pastor had not arrived yet, so the pastor's wife introduced me to the congregation. I started preaching and then I stopped. The Holy Spirit said your pastor is coming in a few minutes. He will be wearing a green suit, and I am to pray for him and say something to him.

Well I started back preaching. A little while later the pastor opened the door. I lost everyone's attention. Every head in the building turned to look at him. You can bet for one reason - to see what color suit he had on. Somehow I knew he had to have a green suit on or I would have to make a new door behind the pulpit wall. Praise the Lord he did have a green suit on. I had no trouble keeping their attention for the rest of the service.

Now getting back to the man I had prayed for and was sitting down beside of. He began to tell me what had happened two weeks ago before when I was there. He said, "You didn't know that I had a lot of money owed to me and that my lawyers just a few days before came and told me I would never get it. When you prayed for me, I said Lord if what he said comes to pass; I will help him to go to India." So as I am sitting there beside of him, as he is weeping, he got his checkbook out and asked me what does it cost for tickets to go to India? I told him and he wrote me a check and gave it to me. I hugged him and prayed for him. I asked the Lord to multiply it back many times over.

My purpose in telling this story and others is for you to still bear in mind, these examples are to encourage you to have faith and stand on the Word. "For God is no respecter of persons." (Romans 2:11) As we prayed for these trips overseas, the first thing the devil said loud and clear was you won't be able to go, you won't get the money. When he says one thing, we tell him he is a liar. We tell him "For with God nothing is impossible." (Luke 1:37) "For my thoughts are not your thoughts, neither are your ways my ways, saith the Lord." (Isaiah 55:8) "The Lord is my rock, and my fortress, and my deliverer, my God, my strength, in whom I will trust, my buckler, and the horn of my salvation and my high tower. I will call upon the Lord, who is worthy to be praised, so shall I be saved from mine enemies."(Psalm 18:2-3)

6
Prayer

Prayer

The Purpose of Prayer

- What is Prayer?
- Benefits of Prayer
- Why Do You Pray?
- Does He Hear our Prayers?

A Command to Pray
Prayers Being Hindered
Waiting and Listening

What is Prayer?

Prayer is the language of the soul speaking to God, through prayer a sinner makes his peace with God. The saint through prayer communes with the Lord.

Things we are to deal with before shipwrecks come our way, not after they come. We are to prepare, be ready before the attacks come. Daniel was prayed up before he went into the lion's den.

I believe one of the most important weapons, we could use to fight the battles of life, when the enemy tries to shipwreck our faith is prayer. Even our Lord and Savior prayed night and day. He taught His disciples to pray, and the importance of prayer.

That is why the enemy fights so hard to interrupt your prayer life.

As we talked about earlier, in order to receive the promises of God's Word, prayer is first along with no unconfessed sin, humbling yourself, die to yourself, fasting, holiness, repentance, obedience, taking up your cross daily, and presenting your bodies as a living sacrifice holy unto the Lord.

You see, prayer is work!!

There are conditions and requirements in getting your prayers answered.

Our spiritual growth doesn't just happen. Just like planting a garden, there are rough rocky soils, brush, roots, even stumps, soil that requires deep plowing, planting, watering and a lot of toiling and hard work to get a good crop. Hey, it's the same, with our walk with the Lord. There's a lot more to it, then just to name and claim it. It doesn't work that way. Prayer is work. Humbling, dying to ones' self, getting self out of the way and bringing the flesh under subjection. Neighbor, it takes perseverance, persistence, getting rid of unbelief, murmuring, bitterness, and breaking up the fallow ground of our hearts and cultivating it to become productive fruit bearers.

Prayer is to take in, to accept, to believe, to meditate, to reflect, to have communion, to be satisfied, to be refreshed, and to be contented. There is no other substitute, or you will end up dissatisfied. Only the spirit and life of Jesus will satisfy the thirsting soul. For me, sometimes it takes the deep dark places for Him to show me something very special. I have found out only He can satisfy me.

He makes sense and purpose out of all I go through. I begin to realize the very special care and attention I receive. I see He wants to lead me. He also wants me to want Him to lead me. Oh neighbor, let the Spirit of God lead and direct you. "That the Lord thy God may shew us the way wherein we may walk, and the things that we may do." (Jeremiah 42:3) "If any man will come after me, let him deny himself, and take up his cross daily and follow me." (Luke 9:23) Today we don't want to do this. We don't want to deny ourselves, or give up our rights to make our own decisions. The problem is we don't want to follow; we want to be the leader. You need to live a life of self denial. "He must increase, but I must decrease." (John 3:30)

I find myself, instead of finding fault with life; it is self and always asking "Why?" I am unwilling to accept every circumstance in an attitude of gratitude. "And we know that all things work together for good to them that love God, to them who are the called according to his purpose." (Romans 8:28)

We are so often quick to forget our blessings and slow to forget our misfortunes! We bring things on ourselves. Example: Prayer is not making deadlines! The Lord tells us, You made the deadlines, I didn't. You meet it.

Our problem is that we set the deadlines for God and try to force Him to meet our deadlines. Disobedience is another, not willing to accept God's Word, God's timing, and taking issue with His will, His authority, and then even questioning His wisdom - this is outright disobedience to Him!

Denying One's Self...Crucified Life

If we would only allow His will to change our will, canceling out all the I's in our decisions, then the cross would finally be applied to our life. And, neighbor, that's the real meaning of taking up our cross daily - to allow the death of one's self, with not our will in the circumstance but His.

Jesus in the Garden of Gethsemane: "Not as I will, but as thou wilt." (Matthew 26:39 42-44) Third time not my will but you Father!

When you don't have a crucified life, you have a side effect of no prayer or prayerlessness. When you don't pray, you become spiritually weak, you become fearful, uneasy, worried, and heavily concerned. You feel like you are carrying the weight of everybody's problems, and you feel responsible even for their problems. You begin to even feel physically, spiritually, and emotionally weak. You forget, greater is He that is in you than he that is in the world.

One of the most important reasons Christians are so weak today is they just don't pray. They are not prepared when the enemy attacks. They go so far as even to listen to the lies of the devil. Such things as prayer aren't important. First of all, you don't have time for it. You think God is too busy, running this universe to fool with little old you. Besides you really shouldn't bother Him.

You see Satan really doesn't want you to trust God. He doesn't want you to let your petitions be known to God by prayer. (Philippians 4:6) Especially he doesn't want you to praise God and thank Him in prayer. When the shipwrecks come, I know my relationship in prayer with God is the very source of <u>my strength</u>!!

Listen, above all the devil doesn't want you to have joy, peace, or strength. He doesn't want you to trust God, or to stand on His promises. You see prayer just doesn't build a foundation but builds layers and layers of faith. You see without faith, it is impossible to please God.

Neighbor, when you don't pray, you get defeated. Prayer is so important, you talk to God, and you listen to God "that the Lord thy God may shew us the way wherein we may walk, and the thing that we may do." (Jeremiah 42:3) In prayer, you ask for wisdom, discernment, healing, protection and guidance. Then you listen to hear, to praise, to give thanks "and thine ears shall hear a word behind thee, saying this is the way, walk ye in it, when ye turn to the right hand and ye turn to the left." (Isaiah 30:21) You need God in your conversations, your experiences, your presence, and your relationships.

Another important aspect of prayer is waiting and listening, to what He speaks to your spirit with a thought, a word, or a verse. "But they that wait upon the Lord shall renew their strength; they shall mount up with wings as eagles; they shall run, and not be weary, and they shall walk, and not faint." (Isaiah 40:31) "Wait on the Lord: be of good courage, and He shall strengthen thine heart: wait I say on the Lord." (Psalm 27:14) "The Lord is good unto them that wait for Him, to the soul that seeketh Him." (Lamentations 3:25)

Prayer is waiting, listening, waiting for His orders to lead you so that you will follow Him and don't try to lead or push Him. Wait for His timetable, not yours. Listen to what He says, through a verse, a word or a thought. He will confirm His word. If He gives you a desire to do something, and you question is this of God? He will increase the desire. He will confirm His word. Through prayer, waiting and listening, the Lord will give you peace about your circumstances. Oh, for the Peace of God! In prayer we get more of God in us, more of His character, His grace, His love, His will, and His holiness. In prayer, we receive our orders from the Master.

Some Benefits of Prayer

Through prayer you are not restless; you are not discontented, agitated, or disturbed. Prayer helps us to prepare for the unexpected, to cope with harsh circumstances. You see in prayer there is the awareness of His presence. Suddenly every thing changes and there is hope, peace, and strength within. He gives reassurance that He is aware of our crises, and He is involved and has it under control. "Oh Lord God! Behold, thou hast made the heaven and the earth by thy great power and stretched out arm, and there is nothing too hard for thee." (Jeremiah 32:17)

Prayer helps us make the right decisions.
Prayer helps us to act and do right.
Prayer helps us to keep the right company.
Prayer gives us strength and energy.
Prayer helps us to have patience.
Prayer helps us to have long suffering.
Prayer helps us to show forgiveness.
Prayer helps us to be fruitful.
Prayer helps us to have the right attitude.
Prayer helps us to have unwavering faith.
Prayer helps us with discernment.

Prayer is my relationship with Jesus. He is the very source of my strength. This relationship is built and established in prayer. We are to move before the enemy attacks us and during the shipwreck with our prayer.

1. **A Command to Pray**

Continue in prayer, and watch in the same with thanksgiving. *(Colossians 4:26)*
Casting all your care upon Him for He careth for you ...by prayer *I Peter 5:7*
Pray without ceasing. *I Thessalonians 5:17*
Night and Day praying exceedingly: *I Thessalonians 3:10*
Watch unto prayer: *I Peter 4:7*
Sick - Pray over him anointing him: *James 5:14*
Prayer of Faith: *James 5:15*
The effectual fervent prayer of a righteous man availeth much: *James 5:16*
Prayer of Agreement: *Matthew 18:19*
Binding and Loosing: *Matthew 18:18*
Petition and Supplication: *Philippians 4:6*
Pray over meals: *Matthew 14:19*
Pray that ye may stand perfect and complete in all the will of God: *Colossians 4:12.*

Humble themselves and pray: *II Chronicles 7:14*

Homework ...For You to Do!!

If you want to be blessed read how important prayer was to:

Prayer of Hezekiah: *II Kings 19:14*
David's prayer of praise: *I Chronicles 29:10*
Jehoshaphat prayer for deliverance: *II Chronicles 20*
Prayer and confession of sin: *Ezra 9:5*
Nehemiah's Prayer: His persistence in prayer Paul's prayer

for knowledge and understanding: *Ephesians 1:15-23*
Hezekiah's prayer for help: *Isaiah 37:14*

2. **Does God Hear Our Prayers?**

"But verily God hath heard me. He hath attended to the voice of my prayers." (Psalm 66:19) "Thou hast given him his heart's desire, and hast not withholden the request of his lips." (Psalm 21:2) "The eyes of the Lord are upon the righteous and His ears are open unto their cry." (Psalm 34:15)

"Behold, the Lord's hand is not shortened, that it couldn't save; neither His ear heavy, that it cannot hear." (Isaiah 59:1)

"The righteous cry and the Lord heareth, and delivereth them out of all their troubles evening, morning, and at noon, will I pray, and cry aloud and He shall hear my voice." (Psalm 55:17) "The Lord is far from the wicked; but He heareth the prayer of the righteous." (Proverbs 15:29) "He shall call upon me, and I will answer him. I will be with him in trouble; I will deliver him." (Psalm 91:15)

"Call unto me, and I will answer thee, and shew thee great and mighty things, which thou knowest not." (Jeremiah 33:3)

"And it shall come to pass that before they call, I will answer and while they are yet speaking I will hear." (Isaiah 65:24)

"The Lord is nigh unto all them that call upon Him, to all that call upon Him in truth." (Psalm 145:18)

Now we know the importance of prayer and that we are commanded to pray. We are told how often to pray. We see the benefits of prayer. We also see that God hears our prayer.

3. **Let's Talk About Our Prayers Being Hindered**

"Likewise, ye husbands, dwell with them according to knowledge, giving honor unto the wife, as unto the weaker vessel, and as being heirs together of the grace of life that your prayer be not hindered." (I Peter 3:7) "Now we know that God hearth not sinners: but if any man be a worshipper of God, and doeth His will, him He hearth." (John 9:31)

"If I regard iniquity in my heart, the Lord will not hear me." (Psalm 66:18) "And when ye stand praying, forgive; if ye have ought against any that your Father also which is in heaven may forgive you your trespasses." (Mark 11:25) "Forbearing one another, and forgiving one another, if any man has a quarrel against any, even as Christ forgave you, so also do ye." (Colossians 3:13)

Hindrances to Getting Your Prayers Answered

Unforgiveness, bitterness, disobedience, rebellion, strife, discord, unbelief, wavering, doubt, unconfessed sin, murmuring, and adultery sin!! Oh neighbor, can't you see how these verses and last categories of sins can be a hindrance in getting your prayers answered and could cause your faith to be shipwrecked? "It's the little foxes that spoil the vines." (Song of Solomon 2:15) It is the same way with sin. Sin is Sin. No black, no white, no big, no little. Sin is Sin!!

As we have looked at prayer and its components or compartments, to be used as a weapon, let's look at another important weapon in our life to be used against the enemy. To keep him from shipwrecking our faith, also bear in mind there is so much more in the Word that the Lord wants to show us. So press on in the Word. "These were more noble than those in Thessalonica, in that they received the word with all readiness of mind and searched the scriptures daily whether those things were so." (Acts 17:11)

Now, perhaps I have said some things, or am going to say something you would answer with "Well, my church doesn't believe in that." It doesn't make any difference what your church believes, or even what I say, it's what the Word says that counts. The Word is for all churches. Even though some are not preaching it!!

Jesus, nor His Word, changes not. "Jesus Christ the same yesterday, and today, and forever." (Hebrews 13:8) "Heaven and earth shall pass away, but my Word shall not pass away." (Matthew 24: 35) "...The words that I speak unto you, they are spirit and they are life." (John 6:63)

7

So Press On Unto Prefection

<u>So Press On Unto Perfection</u>

"Therefore leaving the principles of the doctrine of Christ, let us go on unto perfection; not laying again the foundation of repentance, from dead works, and of faith toward God, of the doctrine of Baptisms, Laying on Hands, Resurrection of the Dead, and of Eternal Judgment." (Hebrews 6:1) Let's look at the word <u>Baptism</u>.

<u>This Holy Spirit Baptism or Filling with the Spirit.</u>

This experience is completely separate from salvation. Let's establish this fact with evidence by the Word, as we look at several places where this took place. Even so some twenty years later after salvation had taken place, church history tells us this happened.

One place was at Ephesus (Acts 19:1-7) "Paul asked them have ye received the Holy Ghost since ye believed? And they said unto him, we have not so much as heard whether there is any Holy Ghost." (Acts 19:2) "And when Paul had laid his hands upon them, the Holy Ghost came on them, and they spoke with tongues and prophesied." (Acts 19:6) You see these were believers that had even been baptized, and didn't receive the Holy Ghost at a baptismal service. You don't get it all once when you are saved. The Holy Spirit and the gifts usually come later, when you ask for them. God is ready to equip you to run this race and will be there for every step of your Christian walk. Hebrews 6:1-2 says let us go on.

Now as we establish evidence along with benefits, why pray in the Spirit? Is it for today? What is the Holy Spirit? We will see how today, the importance of the Holy Spirit is to be used as a weapon when the devil tries to shipwreck your faith! We will learn the importance of praying in the Holy Spirit.

The role the Holy Spirit plays in our lives:

Evidence Filling

"And they were all filled with the Holy Ghost and began to speak with other tongues, as the Spirit gave them utterance." (Acts 2:1-4) Now these were followers that had been with Jesus. There were some followers who had done so for approximately three and a half years. Some of the believers that John the Baptist had baptized, were followers that had denied themselves and taken up their cross daily and followed Jesus. They were with the Master! They had been in Bible College with Professor Jesus and even with all of this, they hadn't received the Holy Ghost as of yet. Now He had breathed on some to receive the Holy Ghost before He left.

Now these were in one accord waiting for the (PROMISE). "And I will pray to the Father, and He shall give you another Comforter, that He may abide with you forever. Even the Spirit of Truth; whom the world cannot receive...(John 14:16-17) (PROMISE) "And behold, I send the promise of my Father, upon you: but tarry ye in the city of Jerusalem, until ye be endued with power from on high." (Luke 24:49) This was part of the Great Commission that He gave just before His ascension. The PROMISE of the Comforter the Holy Spirit filling!

Evidence and Filling

"...that with all boldness they may speak thy word, by stretching forth thine hand to heal, and that signs and wonders may be done by the name of the Holy Child Jesus. And when they had prayed, the place was shaken where they were assembled together, and they were all filled with the Holy Ghost, and they spoke the word of God with boldness." (Acts 4:29-31)

"And Ananias went his way, and entered into the house, and putting his hands on him said, Brother Saul, the Lord, even Jesus, that appeared unto thee in the way as thou comest, hath sent me, that thou mightest receive thy sight, and be filled with the Holy Ghost." (Acts 9:17)

"Also was poured out the gift of the Holy Ghost. For they heard them speak with tongues, and magnify God. Can any man forbid water that these should not be baptized which has received the Holy Ghost as well as us?"

(Acts 10:44-47) Verses 46 & 47 used.
<u>Evidence</u>
<u>Filling</u>
<u>Promise</u>
<u>Benefits, Power</u> Acts 1:8
<u>Teacher</u> John 14:26, I John 2:27
<u>Comforter</u> inner strength John 14: 16 & 17
<u>Power</u> to witness authority Acts 1:8
<u>Gift</u> Receive the gift of the Holy Ghost

For the promise is unto you, and to your children, and to all that are afar off, even as many as the Lord our God shall call. This is for Today, and Forever, for every believer that will ask!

<u>What Is It?</u>

"God is a spirit, and they that worship Him must worship him in Spirit and in Truth." John 4:24

"Likewise the Spirit also helpeth our infirmities: for we know not what we should pray for as we ought: but the spirit itself maketh intercession for us with groaning which cannot be uttered. And He that searcheth the hearts knoweth what is the mind of the Spirit, because He maketh intercession for the saints according to the will of God." (Romans 8:26-27) "The spirit of man is the candle of the Lord, searching all the inward parts of the belly." (Proverbs 20:27)

"For with stammering lips and another tongue will he speak to this people?"

"To whom He said this is the rest wherewith ye may cause the weary to rest; and this is the refreshing: yet they not hear." (Isaiah 28:11-12)

Edification

"But ye, beloved, building up yourselves on your most Holy Faith, praying in the Holy Ghost." (Jude 1:20)

In these verses we see:

The promise is for today and is for you.

We see who the Holy Spirit is and what He does!
We see how we are to worship and pray!
We see the work of the Spirit maketh intercession.
We see the Spirit searching the inward parts of the belly.
We see the rest the Spirit gives!
We see praying in the Spirit builds us up.

Praying in the Spirit or Praying in Tongues is the most powerful way to pray.

Praying in the Spirit allows the Spirit to work out God's will in our lives. The source of our strength is receiving, recognizing, and relying on the Holy Spirit and to be immersed and energized in the Holy Spirit.

The Holy Spirit makes me feel and sense the presence of Jesus. He brings me quietness, serenity, strength and peace in the midst of frustrations and problems. He brings healing answers to difficult problems, far greater than I imagined. "Now unto Him that is able to do exceeding abundantly above all that we ask or think, according to the power that worketh in us."(Ephesians 3:20) "...John indeed baptized with water but ye shall be baptized with the Holy Ghost." (Acts 11:16)

You need this power; this prayer language to help you when the devil tries to shipwreck your faith. A language that gets self out of the way when you pray. A language that the devil can't understand or interfere with!

Now there are hindrances to keep you from receiving the Holy Spirit: Unbelief, doubt or not yielding your mind and spirit.

There are two basic requirements in receiving the Holy Spirit:

> Obedience - knowing Jesus as your Savior and having presented your body. Holy. "And we are His witnesses of these things: and so is also the Holy Ghost, whom God hath given to him that obeys Him." (Acts 5:32) "If ye then, being evil know how to give good gifts unto your children: how much more shall your Heavenly Father give the Holy Spirit to them that ask him." (Luke 11:11-13)

Salvation is for all but only those who repent, confess and believe when they call on the name of Jesus! The Holy Spirit is for all, but one has to ask, yield and receive.

Now pray with me, Lord Jesus, I ask you now to baptize me in the Holy Spirit. Fill me to overflowing with your spirit! I surrender everything within me, to your control, and I receive this gift by faith. I receive from you a prayer language, so that I can praise you in a new way. Thank you for giving me this new gift. I use my mind, tongue. I thank you for this strange pressure, utterance that's bubbling (boils) up within my innermost being demanding expression. I feel a bubbling faith of living water down inside me with a phrase of words that are coming forth. Praise you and thank you. "He that believeth on me, as the scripture hath said, out of his belly shall flow rivers of living water." (John 7:38)

I pray you now see the importance of how to use the Holy Spirit for many reasons in our life and what a very special weapon this can be used in your life when shipwrecks come.

8
Spiritual Gifts

Spiritual Gifts

Now let's look at what goes along with the Holy Spirit. Let's think about another component or compartment:

Spiritual Gifts That Glorify God

"Now concerning spiritual gifts, Brethren, I would not have you ignorant." (I Corinthians 12:1)

Nine Gifts of the Spirit:

Revelation Gifts:
- The Word of Wisdom
- The Word of Knowledge
- Discerning of Spirits

Voice Gifts
- Tongues
- Interpretation
- Prophecy

Power Gifts
- Faith
- Healing
- Miracles

Distribution of the Gifts

"But all these worketh that one and the selfsame spirit, dividing to every man severally as He will." (I Corinthians 12:11)

Gifts

These gifts are given to the body of Christ so that they may profit from them and edify Jesus Christ.

Revelation Gifts

The Word of Wisdom, first of all, it proclaims, it declares wisdom in the time of need for a particular problem, and it is a special revelation of the Spirit. It also draws from God's wisdom but the wisdom that is from above is first pure, then peaceable gentle and easy to be intreated, full of mercy and good fruit. (James 3:17)

A Word of Knowledge

Knowledge that has to do with the knowledge of God and is not the words man's wisdom teacheth, but which the Holy Ghost teacheth to lead, to guide, to give you the answer to your need, for the needs at hand. "Answers" (Facts)

Discerning of Spirit

"Beloved, believe not every spirit, but try the spirits whether they are of God; because many false prophets are gone out into the world." (I John 4:1) Distinguish between good and evil spirits. Perception is the person of God, for real, or false. Test them with the Word. Do you bear witness to what they say and do? Neighbor, it's a specific gift that we need in this world today with the way some people are or pretend to be - especially with the many cults and different denominations in this world today that some are not of God!

Voice Gifts

Tongues

I Corinthians 14: "Speaking in tongues is communication, prayer languages to our Heavenly Father, which Satan cannot understand." That's the main reason why he fights so hard to keep people from receiving this gift. Tongues are mentioned in a number of books in the Bible - Acts, Corinthians 14, Isaiah 28:11 and Romans 8: 26-27. When we pray in tongues the Spirit prays. (I Corinthians 14:14-15) (See Evidence and Filling)

Interpretation

Thus the contents or interpretation of the message in tongues. The interpreter puts in words the meaning of the message. The interpretation comes from the Holy Spirit to edify the church. Now this act requires faith on one's part because sometimes only a few words are given to the individual, then as he starts in faith, the rest comes given by the Spirit's utterance.

Prophecy

"And it shall come to pass afterwards that I will pour out my spirit upon all flesh; and your sons and your daughters shall prophecy, your old men shall dream dreams, your young men shall see visions." (Joel 2:28) Wherefore, Brethren, covet to prophesy and forbid not to speak with tongues." (I Corinthians 14:39) Paul encouraged us to seek prophecy. Prophecy also touches privacy even in areas of people's lives. Revealing secrets also brings convictions and encouragement. It tells of events to take place in days ahead.

Power Gifts

Faith

"Now faith is the substance of things hoped for, the evidence of things not seen." (Hebrews 11:1) "Through faith we understand that the worlds were framed by the Word of God so that things which are seen were not made of things which do appear." (Hebrews 11:3) Now you read

Hebrews 11 and see the example of the patriarchs; Abraham, Moses, and others and the example of prophets and judges and other people of faith.

Now faith is simply, complete trust, believing, and standing on the Word. What is faith?

Faith is a mountain mover.
Faith is a way maker.
Faith works miracles.
Faith is a gift.
Faith is a shield to quench the fiery darts of the enemy.

The gift of faith could be the impartation of faith itself to the believer and gives us power to carry out God's Word. We are justified by faith. We have access by faith to God. "So then faith cometh by hearing, and hearing cometh by the Word of God." (Romans 10:17) We please God by faith. "But without faith it is impossible to please Him: for he that cometh to God must believe that He is, and that He is a rewarder of them that diligently seek Him." (Hebrews 11:6) Now fear, doubt and unbelief is opposite of faith. Doubt and go without, believe and receive! Have faith!!

To another the gift of healing by the same Spirit and faith is another component. One of the first recorded miracles of the early church was a lame man healed! Example: Peter and John had the gift of healing. Peter and John went into the temple at the hour of prayer. A lame man was laid at the gate. He asked for alms from people entering the temple. He looked up to see Peter and John and asked them for alms. Peter looked into his eyes and said look at John and me. You are looking expecting some silver and gold, we don't have any, but such as I have given to thee in the name of Jesus Rise and walk. Immediately his feet and ankle bones received strength and he took off, leaping and walking. (Acts 3:1-10)

The New Testament is full of examples of the gift of healing. I myself have been healed many times by the gift of healing. It is a gift that heals at a particular time and is a gift to be used for sick, afflicted people. Today people like Oral Roberts, and the late Katherine Kuhlman had this gift. The Spirit supplies the ministry of healing. It's the power that flowed (Holy Ghost) shot into the sick person. This gift is for today for the body of Christ.

<u>The Gift of Working of Miracles</u>

Is similar to the gift of healing! Examples: Working of miracles in finances, life threatening issues, or domestic problems.

Working of miracles is a supernatural power above and beyond anything man can do. "For with God nothing shall be impossible." (Luke 1:37)

"The things which are impossible with men are possible with God." (Luke 18:27)

Miracles defeat Satan's plans. "Now God anointed Jesus of Nazareth with the Holy Ghost and with power: who went about doing well and healing all that were oppressed of the devil. For God was with Him." (Acts 10:8) The working of miracles show Jesus power is greater! ..."Greater is He that is in you than he that is in the world." (I John 4:4) It is my prayer that you will see the importance of these gifts, to fight against the enemy when he tries to shipwreck your faith and also see the need of these gifts for every day use.

Power for service comes through the gifts and fruit of the Spirit.

Bear in mind, we must come together, the same as the parts of our physical body. No member (part) of our body is not important.

Each gift functions - all are important. Just like in the church. "And He gave some apostles and some prophets, and some evangelists, and some pastors and teachers." (Ephesians 4:11) Now just like He gave all these different leaders, one is just as important as the other. Along with the gifts one is important as the other to work together to function in the church and in each life to edify, clarify, and magnify the Lord Jesus Christ! Paul says don't be ignorant about the gifts but to covet earnestly the gifts. These gifts are so important to have to use against the enemy when he tries to shipwreck your faith.

The Holy Spirit is stronger than the devil and the gifts of the Spirit provide the power to defeat the devil. Paul, that Holy Ghost preacher, who turned every street corner into a pulpit, declared that Jesus Christ is Lord. The man who wrote half of the New Testament tells us to desire spiritual gifts, and tells us in I Corinthians 14:5, "I wish you all would speak in tongues and prophesy." Covet the gifts in I Corinthians 12: to overcome and defeat the enemy when shipwrecks come. Now along with the Holy Spirit, the gifts to use as a weapon, let's look at another component or compartment that goes hand and hand with these.

[illegible]

9

The Fruit of the Spirit

The Fruit of the Spirit

The gifts are of no value unless exercised in love. The fruits of the Spirit can more accurately be described as traits developing in Christian character and qualities in the Christian.

Love

Fruit of the Spirit can only begin with love and is completed in love. This love is the same kind of love God gave at Calvary. "For God so loved the world that He gave His only begotten son, that whosoever believeth in Him should not perish but have everlasting life." (John 3:16) God gave His Son for you and I, even while we were still sinners. We are to show forth love, not just in saying, but in doing. Love is an action.

Joy

We are to have continuous joy. "Rejoice in the Lord always: and again I say Rejoice." (Philippians 4:4) Now someone might be thinking right now or perhaps is saying Joy, Joy, you are not married to him or her but I am!!! Now take it by faith! Ask the Lord to give you strength. "...neither be sorry: for the joy of the Lord is your strength." (Nehemiah 8:10) Remember always - "A merry heart doeth good like a medicine, but a broken spirit drieth the bones." (Proverbs 17:22) True joy says you have a right relationship with the Lord.

Peace

"The Lord will give strength unto His people; the Lord will bless His people with peace." (Psalm 29:11) You can have peace even while you sleep. "I will both lay me down in peace, and sleep; for thou, Lord only maketh me dwell in safety." (Psalms 4:8) Peace - "Thou wilt keep him in perfect peace, whose mind is stayed on thee: because he trusteth in thee." (Isaiah 26:3) Peace of heart and mind. "Peace I leave with you, my peace I give unto you: not as the world giveth, give I unto you. Let not your heart be troubled, neither let it be afraid." (John 14:27) You want to have and keep peace in your life? Apply these verses. "Finally, Brethren, whatsoever things are true, whatsoever things are honest, whatsoever things are just, whatsoever things are pure, whatsoever things are lovely, and whatsoever things are of good report. If there be any virtue, and if there be any praise, think on these things. Those things, which ye have both learned, and received, and heard, and seen in me, do: and the God of Peace shall be with you." (Philippians 4:8-9) Finally, real peace comes from the Holy Spirit. It takes love and joy working through the Spirit to develop the rest of the fruits!

Longsuffering

Having patience with those who try to aggravate, or upset you to make you angry. James says "Wherefore my beloved brethren, let every man be swift to hear, slow to speak, slow to wrath."(1:19) "With all lowliness and meekness, with longsuffering, forbearing one another in love." (Ephesians 4:2) Paul's life and example: "But thou hast fully known my doctrine, manner of life, purpose, faith, longsuffering, charity, and patience." (II Timothy 3:10) Paul charges us to have longsuffering. "Preach the word; be instant in season, out of season; reprove, rebuke, exhort with all long suffering and doctrine." (II Timothy 4:2)

Gentleness

David's Song of Deliverance

"...and thy gentleness hath made me great." (II Samuel 22:36) Gentleness - is kindness towards one another. It also enables one to give a soft answer at all times and to avoid the other person's anger.

Goodness

Goodness - Morally excellent, honorable worth, a good reputation, generous, loving kindness, good manners, pleasant, suitable, being good, and having excellence of character. "The fruit of the spirit is in all goodness and righteousness and truth" (Ephesians 5:9) "...The goodness of God lendeth thee to repentance." (Romans 2:4) "Behold therefore the goodness and severity of God on them which fell, severity, but toward thee goodness if thou continue in His goodness. Otherwise thou shall be cut off." (Romans 11:22)

Faith

See the nine gifts of the Spirit,
Power Gift Faith

Meekness

Having a patient, gentle disposition. Gentle, soft. Meekness is not putting others down. Meekness is true pure humility. One that doesn't think he is too good to do just any task that's set before him. Paul charges us to follow after meekness! "But thou, O, man of God, flee thee things; and follow after righteousness, godliness, faith, love, patience, meekness." (I Timothy 6:11) Titus tells us to show meekness to all men. "To speak evil of no man, to be no brawlers, but gentle, showing all meekness unto all men." (Titus 3:2)

Temperance

Temperance - self control. Now in developing self control, we take care of and control desires, impurities, passions, while the Holy Spirit enables us to discipline ourselves. Now you have to cooperate with the Spirit in obedience to allow the disciplining of ourselves if we are to grow spiritually.

Daily we have to cultivate, break up, and turn over the fallow ground of our hearts in order for the fruit to grow. We have to daily die to self. We have to circumcise ourselves to the Lord and take away the foreskins of our hearts and let the fruits be manifested in our lives!

Oh how we need to let these fruits grow and develop in us, so we can have love, joy, peace, longsuffering, gentleness, goodness, faith, meekness and temperance. Along with these is victory, contentment, faith, which are activated in us by the Spirit.

The Spirit is there to help us while we patiently endure wrongs or difficulties that come our way. We can have peace while others have strife, division and discord.

Now after we have looked at the fruits. Are they in full operating fruition in your life? Perhaps there are some cracks, flaws, potholes in your spiritual walk that need adjustments, or perhaps repentance needs to take place. If so, ask the Lord to help you see the importance of these fruits and gifts to be in your life for when the shipwrecks come.

10

Spiritual Armor - Spiritual Welfare

Spiritual Armor

Christians are in a real spiritual battle with the forces of darkness daily. "And from the days of John the Baptist until now the kingdom of heaven suffereth violence and the violent take it by force." (Matthew 11:12) These consist of principalities, powers and the rulers of the darkness of this world and spiritual wickedness that take place.

Christians have to stay focused - be alert, stand guard, and be aware that, "the thief cometh not, but for to steal and to kill, and to destroy." (John 10:10) One reason God sent His Son, Jesus of Nazareth, and anointed Him with the Holy Ghost, and with power was so He would destroy the works of the devil and heal all that were oppressed of Him! (Acts 10:38) "Then Jesus said, I have to go be with my Father. I want to tell you about the power of authority and unlimited power I am giving you. The works I have been doing, you will be doing them and also greater works because I am going home to be with my Father." (John 14:12)

So after I am gone you are going to need to be on guard at all times. He can attack you anytime, any place, no matter where or when. Don't wait until he shows up for the battle to get prepared. Be prepared and dressed so he doesn't shipwreck your faith!

Don't ever think you are immune from attack. One of the biggest reasons the enemy defeats Christians is because they go around streaking - not dressed with spiritual armor.

Spiritual armor really is the nature and likeness of Jesus. If we put power and righteousness on, we fully obey and trust Him as we look to Him. His armor provides complete protection from all kinds of evil strategies, attacks and tricks of the devil.

This Christian life is sometimes a struggle. It requires a number of factors, as I have mentioned in earlier chapters, in receiving the wisdom and strength to make the right decisions in using the armor, prayer and the Word to defeat the devil!

The devil will try to use his forces of evil to blind even Christians. To doubt the Lord and defeat them, but they are not adequate or powerful enough against the Lord. This is why Christians that struggle in their own strength to make it, will fail.

Spiritual Armor = Spiritual Warfare. In Ephesians 6:10-18, we see Paul's application and purpose for a Christian soldier. Spiritual Armor is the equipment for the battle in warfare against spiritual enemies.

We are to be dressed for the battle even though the battle is the Lord's. Just like when God told Jehoshaphat "For the battle is not yours; but God's." (II Chronicles 20:15) Paul charged us to be a good soldier of Jesus Christ. (II Timothy 2:3) Paul continuously alludes to the fact of the equipment of the soldier in many places in the New Testament. Telling us "Putting on the breastplate of faith and love: and for a helmet, the hope of salvation." (I Thessalonians 5:8) Now this warfare in general is between saints and evil spirits that are against God, wicked spirits of Satan in the heavenlies. Even though the battle is the Lord's, we still have to participate in the battle. Just like Moses, Joshua, Jehoshaphat, and Old Testament prophets and saints. Hebrews 11 tells of a good example of all the patriarchs.

Spiritual Warfare

Ephesians 6:10: Notice in this warfare, we are commanded steps to take, and what steps to do with equipment to put on. First, be strong in the Lord and in His power and might. Notice His - not ours. "I can do all things through Christ which strengthen me." (Philippians 4:13) You see spiritual strength, courage and wisdom is needed for the warfare: being strong for His cause, His Word, His kingdom, increasing in His strength, His power, and His wisdom. Allow the Spirit to take control while we stand, abide, and trust Him.

Verse 11 - We have to be armed from head to toe, front and back. As we use all our defenses and weapons, we liken this spiritual armor as a hedge of protection around about us. Similarly, liken this to the equipment of police, firemen, and soldiers as warfare for everyday battle. With the armor on, it prepares and completes and enables us to stand against all assaults and forces of the devil. In putting on this armor, we cover over the flesh, and our ability. We are to wear His armor day and night.

Verse 12 - We stand against powers of darkness, and not human enemies. Satan's forces, liken to a kingdom of darkness where our Lord's kingdom is light, peace, and everlasting. Satan's kingdom consists of wicked spirits which attack us to cause doubt, fear, and discouragement, disbelief to destroy our relationship with the Lord, and our walk with Him, and causes us to miss out on Heaven.

Verse 13 - Take the whole armor of God that ye may be able to withstand the evil days. Stand, abide, rest, trust, and wait as we stand in Him on His Word. Complete reliance that He is able to do exceeding, abundantly above all we ask or think.

Verse 14 - Still standing having your loins girt about with truth and having on the breastplate of righteousness. Notice loins - procreating power - reproduce to beget to produce. Bring into being. Verse 14 - girt about with truth. "Jesus saith unto him, I am the way, the truth and the life. No man cometh unto the Father but by me." (John 14:6) and having on the breastplate of righteousness. Breastplate -armor for the body in warfare on the breast. It is also worn by the Jewish High Priest. (II Chronicles 20)

Righteousness - An act of God, where man is made just or free from the guilt or penalty of sin, truthfulness. "And righteousness shall be the girdle of his lions, and faithfulness the girdle of his reins." (Isaiah 11:5) Resisting - Temptation, wrong thinking, and righteousness - is to take care of our emotions, our attitudes and our responses. As we put fourth meekness, long suffering, temperance, gentleness, and faith. In righteousness, we express these traits. As proofs of our spiritual life, Paul exhorts us - "Let this mind be in you, who was also in Christ Jesus." (Philippians 2:5) God desires truth in our innermost being. Our mind should be fortified with truth. The righteousness of the Word is a breastplate to fortify our hearts from the attacks of Satan. Righteousness will help us to walk in obedience to the command of God's Word.

Verse 15 - Your feet shod with the preparation of the gospel of peace. Peace is the very foundation in our walk with the Lord. "Thou will keep him in perfect peace whose mind is stayed on thee because he trusteth in thee." (Isaiah 26:3) Having confidence and courage, trust, everlasting strength and assurance and saying I will take up my cross and follow wherever He leads or directs me! Peace inables me to stand firm on and in the Word. Because "Greater is He that is in me than he that is in the world." (I John 4:4) With this assurance we stand with no fear in our minds or heart. Peace is able use to make the right decisions so our faith won't be shipwrecked.

Feet shod with preparation of the gospel of peace. Preparation - as we study to show thyself approved unto God, a workman that needeth not to be ashamed, rightly dividing the Word of Truth. That we would be sanctified in the Lord's Word and always be ready to give an answer of the hope that is in you, the Word.

Realizing "how beautiful are the feet of them that preach the gospel of peace and bring glad tidings of good things." (Romans 10:15)

Preparation - prepare, provide, make ready. Peace -

quietness, rest, freedom from strife, discomfort, mental and disobedience. Anguish - despair, and opposition of the wicked one. Gospel - good news, glad tidings, and your feet shod wit the preparation of the gospel of peace! Verse 15.

"Above all taking the shield of faith, where with ye shall be able to quench all the fiery darts of the wicked." Verse 16 Faith is the shield God gives us as a weapon to use in the battle of life. Faith is also an action, a force, a conviction. Faith is a walk, a belief, an assurance of trust. "For we walk by faith not by sight." (II Corinthians 5:7) "Now faith is the substance of things hoped for the evidence of things not seen." (Hebrews 11:1) Faith is the victory He gives us to overcome the forces of darkness. Faith is what God desires for us to have in pleasing Him. "But he that cometh to God must believe that He is, and that He is a rewarder of them that diligently seek Him." (Hebrews 11:6) You see you can't please Him unless you have faith.

We must come to Him in faith believing, trusting, and knowing. Believe and receive, doubt and go without. In faith, it is one means of receiving His rewards? Faith puts bad thoughts out and good ones in. Faith takes care of the spirit, heart, soul and mind. (Verse 16) Faith quenches the fiery parts of the wicked; He extinguishes and puts them out. Faith is a gift we are all given a measure of. We go from faith to faith. In obedience, as we willingly yield to the Lord our self discipline. Faith is our shield!

"For whatsoever is born of God overcometh the world and this is the victory that overcometh the world even our faith." (I John 5:4) and take the helmet of salvation - the helmet protects the head and keeps the soul purified and not defiled by attacks of the enemy to the mind.

We use and fill our minds with things that are true, honest, just, and lovely. In doing this, we allow the peace of God to keep our minds thinking God's thoughts. With our spiritual helmet on ,we can stand against evil, hurtful, wicked, and deceitful thoughts.

The sword of the Spirit which is the Word of God. Verse 17 -"...Word of God is quick and powerful, and sharper than any two-edged sword." (Hebrews 4:12) " HisWord is spirit and life." (John 6:63) "The words of the Lord are pure words, as silver tried in a furnace of earth, purified seven times."(Psalm 12:6) "Heaven and earth shall pass away, but my words shall not pass away." (Matthew 24:25)

In these verses we see how powerful, pure, quick, lasting, the Word of God is, and to be used because it is spirit and life. It is going to be here forever. God give us this weapon to overpower and conquer the devil with, so use it as He did."

11

Renewing Your Mind

Renewing Your Mind

"I beseech you therefore, brethren, by the mercies of God, that ye present your bodies a living sacrifice, holy, acceptable unto God, which is your reasonable service and be not conformed to this world; but be ye transformed by the renewing of your mind, that ye may prove what is the good and acceptable and the perfect will of God." (Romans 12:1-2) and Jesus answered him, "The first of all the commandments is hear, O Israel; the Lord our God is one Lord. And thou shall love the Lord thy God with all thy heart, and with all thy soul, and with all thy mind, and with all thy strength. This is the first commandment." (Mark 12: 29-30)

Notice in Romans 12: 1-2 that in living the Christian life, we are to be a living sacrifice. We are to be holy, acceptable unto God in service to Him. In being holy, a sanctification work has to be done in us. He tells us don't be conformed to this world. "Wherefore come out from among them, and be ye separate, saith the Lord, and touch not the unclean things, and I will receive you." (II Corinthians 6:17) The Apostle Paul tells us about being separate and not conformed to this world. James tells us even further about worldliness, pride, lust and greed. He says "ye adulters and adulteresses, know ye not that the friendship of the world is enemy with God? Whosoever therefore will be a friend of the world is the enemy of God." (James 4:4)

So as Christians, we are to be transformed by the renewing of our minds so that we can know what the good and perfect will of God is in our lives. Even today so many of God's children, saints, don't press in to see what His perfect will is. "Beloved I wish above all things that thou mayest prosper and be in health, even as thy soul prospereth." (III John 2) His will is His Word. Notice in being separate, pressing into His Word, "That the Lord thy God may shew us the way wherein we may walk, and the things that we may do." (Jeremiah 42:3) Showing us and telling us His will in our lives by renewing our mind with His Word.

Now if one was to ask the purpose - reason, necessity, benefit, desire in renewing the mind, let's talk about the arena of the mind.

In Ephesians 6:16 it says with the shield of faith, we are to quench all the fiery darts of the wicked. Darts of bad thoughts of fear, frustration, worry, doubt, confusion, discouragement, anger and unforgiveness, etc.,(all of which are contrary to the Word of God). The devil sends thoughts to try and control our minds to cause havoc with anything, and everything, to break, disrupt our relationship, and our intimacy, with the Lord. The devil also sends thoughts that would cause you to be disobedient to the Father!

"For lo the wicked bent their bow, they make ready their arrow upon the string, that they may privily shoot at the upright in heart. If the foundations be destroyed, what can the righteous do?" (Psalm 11: 2-3)

We have looked at spiritual armor and the importance of each piece. As we were commanded to put it on, wear it. To defeat the enemy and the benefits of wearing it so Satan couldn't shipwreck our faith. His Word tells us in Hebrews 6:1 "Let us go on to perfection....."We see in the Word that righteousness of God is revealed from faith to faith. As we walk in a little light then a little more is revealed. "For precept must be upon precept, precept upon precept; line upon line, line upon line, here a little, and there a little." (Isaiah 28:10)

You don't receive all the knowledge of God and His Word at salvation. We are to increase in the grace and knowledge of the Lord. Daily ask Him to give us more wisdom and revelation of His Word. Paul told the Philippians "let this mind be in you which was also in Christ Jesus." Verse 2:5

In essence a whole book could be written on the necessity, benefit, and purpose of renewing your mind. Let's look at some main reasons that would help us to benefit.

Purpose of Renewing Your Mind

1. To rid - clean out Satan's programming and eradicate Satan's programming. II Thessalonians 2:2 "...

that ye be not soon shaken in mind." Romans 8:5-8 notice Verse 7. "The carnal mind is the enemy against God." Romans 12:"... and be not conformed to this world. But be ye transformed by the renewing of your mind, that ye may prove what is that good and acceptable and perfect will of God."

2. To destroy Satan's demon control and replace bad thoughts, with, "whatsoever things are pure whatsoever things are lovely, whatsoever things are of good report; if there be any virtue, and if there be any praise, think on these things."

The arena of the mind is Satan's access which is his main battleground to try and inject and control our thoughts. Now we can't stop him from sending those thoughts. We are responsible for bringing our thoughts into subjection and replacing them with God's thoughts. "For I know the thoughts that I think toward you, saith the Lord. Thoughts of peace, and not of evil, to give you an expected end." (Jeremiah 29:11) When thoughts or attacks come against you in the arena of the mind, think what does the Word say? And use it just like Jesus did in Matthew 4:4 so Satan doesn't shipwreck your faith. As John 16:13 says:

"Always speak in line with and do what the Word says."

3. Purpose of Renewing Your Mind: To strengthen your ability to obey the Word of God. "He said yea rather blessed are they that hear the Word of God and keep it." (Luke 11:28) "But be doers of the word and not hearers only." (James 1:22)

Obedience is one word from Genesis to Revelation that can not be replaced. Obedience is one word that brings the blessing of God.

4. Purpose of Renewing Your Mind: Life in the Spirit results in <u>deliverance from sin</u>. <u>No condemnation</u> to those who walk not after the flesh, but after the Spirit. Remember Satan always condemns, but God convicts! To eliminate demonic strongholds, the unrenewed mind is an open target.

5. Purpose of Renewing Your Mind: To remove, omit, drive out the possibility of deception. "Beloved, believe not every spirit, but try the spirits whether they are of God; because many false prophets are gone out into the world." (I John 4:4)

<u>Steps to Take to Renew Your Mind</u>

a. Casting Down! Bringing into Captivity!
b. How we Walk!
c. What Does it Mean to Faint in Your Mind?
d. Received the Word How?
e. Readiness of Mind

"For though we walk in the flesh, we do not war after the flesh: For the weapons of our warfare are not carnal, but mighty through God to the pulling down of stronghold; casting down, imaginations, and every high thing that exalted itself against the knowledge of God and bringing into captivity every thought to the obedience of Christ. (II Corinthians 10:3 4-5)

a. Casting Down

Casting down every high thing, and bringing into captivity every thought. In Jesus' teaching on prayer "But thou, when thou prayest, enter into thy closet, and when thou hast shut thy door, pray to thy Father which is in secret and thy Father which seeth in secret shall reward thee openly." (Matthew 6:6) In the arena of the mind, one of Satan's main battlegrounds, is especially when you try to shut the door to your mind. You turn the stereo, TV, or radio off. You take these actions, steps to close yourself off to be in His presence. The telephone rings twice as loud as it regularly does. Nobody has called you until now! The doorbell rings. Along with this taking place, while you are shut in with the Lord, all these thoughts come to your mind about what you need to do, where you have to go! You are alone with many other thoughts that are contrary to the Word of God. At this point, you have to cast down, bring every thought that would interfere with your prayers to the obedience of Christ. Realize the power of authority that you as a believer have over your thoughts.

"Verily I say unto you, whatsoever ye bind on earth shall be bound in heaven. And whatsoever you loose on earth shall be loosed in heaven." (Matthew 18:18) You have power to cancel out thoughts or to entertain them. As you cast down every bad thought and bring it into captivity as you also bind bad thoughts and replace them with good ones."(Philippians 4:8)

b. How We Walk

In this Christian walk, we need to keep our minds renewed with evidences of truly knowing God. "And hereby we do know that we know Him, if we keep His commandments. He that saith, I know Him, and keepeth not His commandments, is a liar, and truth is not in him. But whoso keepeth His Word, in him verily is the Love of God perfected; hereby know we that we are in Him. He that saith He abideth in Him ought himself also to walk even as He walked. (I John 2: 3-6) Now don't talk the talk, if you are not walking the walk. The purpose of renewing your mind is to walk as Jesus walked on this earth. Walk as He walked, with instant forgiveness, unconditional love, an upward look and with compassion. He forgave Judas, He forgave His murders, He forgave Peter who denied him, Thomas who doubted Him and He will forgive you if you will let Him. Are you walking as He did, so your faith won't be shipwrecked?

c. What Does It Mean to Faint in Your Mind?

"For consider him that endured such contradiction of sinners against himself, lest ye be wearied and faint in your minds." (Hebrews 12:3) Faint in your minds = reverse of joy, cheerful, weary, exhausted, despondent, and sinking of spirit, through power of difficulty and opposition. Result is partial or complete abandonment of vows, promises, and one's stand for the Lord and His Word. In transforming you will renew your mind. By application as "These were more noble than those in Thessalonica, in that they received the word with all readiness of mind, and searched the scriptures daily, whether those things were so." (Acts 17:11)

d. Received the Word How?

With readiness of mind. How do you receive the Word? Do you look into your Bible as a mirror to see how you stand up to His Word in faithfulness, truthfulness, obedience, in your walk, and in your talk? Do you pray even before you read and make sure there would be no hindrance in getting your prayers answered? Readiness is to hear His voice. To receive His orders, of love, rebuke, chasten! Readiness - Did you pray for your Pastor to receive a fresh word, not only for you but for others for their needs to be met? Readiness means going to bed early, getting proper rest, and cutting the television off. Fresh to receive and to be a blessing to others.

e. Readiness of Mind

"Search the Scriptures daily, whether those things were so. " (Acts 17:11) "And He said unto them, take heed what ye hear." (Mark 4.24) "Take heed therefore how ye hear..."(Luke 8:18) "My people are destroyed for lack of knowledge." (Hosea 4:6) "Therefore my people are gone into captivity because they have no knowledge."(Isaiah 5:13) First for lack of knowledge, we don't receive the blessing of the Lord even in receiving our heavenly home. Without renewing our mind and putting on spiritual armor, we can be defeated. Sadly to say, Christians today listen a lot to what sounds good and what feels good! They hear some Dr. Fahrenheit or some famous person, say something that makes it right. He doesn't say anything about holiness, repentance, being separate, or right living. Further, he doesn't back it up with Genesis to Revelation. It's his opinion. "Jesus said my words are spirits and life." (John 6:63) "Because they don't search the scriptures daily, they fall prey to some cult or denomination that doesn't believe in the Father, Son and Holy Ghost." (I John 5:7) "And there is no way to the Father except through the Son." (Acts 4:12) Please renew your mind by searching the scriptures daily so Satan won't shipwreck your faith.

In Renewing Your Mind

Here are some further steps to take in renewing your mind:

1. We are to love the Lord with all our heart, soul and <u>with all our mind</u>.
2. Not have a doubtful <u>mind</u>.
3. Receive the Word with all readiness of <u>mind</u>.
4. Serve the Lord with all humility of <u>mind</u>.
5. Let every man be fully persuaded in his own <u>mind</u>.
6. Be perfectly joined together in the same <u>mind</u>.
7. For if there be first a willing <u>mind</u>.
8. Not soon shaken in <u>mind</u>.
9. Be not wearied and faint in your <u>mind</u>.
10. Stir up your pure <u>mind</u>.
11. Be renewed in the spirit of your <u>mind</u>.
12. Be transformed by the renewing of your <u>mind</u>.

Now you search the scriptures out and let the Holy Spirit say what else you need to see the importance of Romans 12:2. " Renew your mind so that Satan doesn't shipwreck your faith."

A Final Word and Prayer

As I have said in the beginning about this book, I am writing to the least, the lonely and the lost, praying that it would help to increase your faith, your confidence and your trust in the Lord and that it would be of comfort and encouragement to you. For you to see and realize "but without faith it is impossible to please Him: for He that cometh to God must believe that He is, and that He is a rewarder of them that diligently seek Him." (Hebrews 11:6)

Our ultimate goal is to seek and to find the holiness that leads us into the presence of God. We must be perfectly consecrated, wholly set apart for Jesus!

My Prayer for You and Your Family

Oh Father, in the name of Jesus, we enter your courts with praise and thanksgiving, blessing your Holy, Holy name. Oh how I pray that you would be filled to the fullest with knowledge, with wisdom and with spiritual understanding to know His will to be strengthened by His Spirit in the inner man, and that you would walk grounded in His love. I pray that you will give praise and glory to Him in all things and know that with Him it's never, never too late with Him. With God, all things are possible, oh how He is able to do exceedingly and abundantly far, far above even all that we ask or think, that you would hold fast to Him with confidence, rejoicing with hope firm to the end.

Oh how I pray that the Lord would show you the way you must walk and the things He wants you to do. I pray that you would hear His voice saying this is the right way you need to turn left for awhile, and then go right. In doing so, you might have to go through some deep water, oh but I will be with you. It won't overflow you, there might be some hot fires you have to go through but listen they won't burn you. Oh how I pray as you know many afflictions will come upon you but I will delivereth you out of them all. Father, right now I pray for each one that has read this book for you to meet their spiritual, physical and financial needs. I just plead the blood of Jesus over their lives, their family and their love ones. I pray in the name of Jesus and the help of the Holy Spirit as they wear their spiritual armor and walk with the gifts of the spirit and the fruits of the spirit in their life for a hedge of protection around about them in the name of Jesus. I speak peace, contentment, faith, victory, health, joy and that He would increase and we would decrease.

I want to thank you very much for reading this book - To God Be the Glory - please add me to your prayer list.